LET THE PARTY BEGIN!

RISE AND RECLAIM YOUR LOST DOMINION:
THE PRINCIPLES FOR A NEW BEGINNING

Dr. Femi Olorunnisola

ISBN 979-8-88685-647-7 (paperback)
ISBN 979-8-88685-648-4 (digital)

Christian Faith Publishing
832 Park Avenue
Meadville, PA 16335
www.christianfaithpublishing.com

Unless otherwise indicated, all Scripture references are from the King James Version (KJV) of the Holy Bible.

Verses marked TLB are taken from The Living Bible, copyright © 1971. Used by permission of Tyndale House Publishers Inc., Wheaton, Illinois 60189. All rights reserved.

Verses marked NLT are taken from Holy Bible, New Living Translation, copyright © 1996, 2004, 2015, by Tyndale House Foundation. Used by permission of Tyndale House Publishers Inc., Carol Stream, Illinois 60188. All rights reserved.

Verses marked TPT are taken from The Passion Translation®, copyright © 2017, 2018, 2020, by Passion & Fire Ministries Inc. Used by permission. All rights reserved. thePassionTranslation.com.

This book was published for Insight Books Publications, an imprint of Femi Olorunnisola teaching and writing ministries.

Maya Angelou "Still I Rise" from *And Still I Rise: A Book of Poems.* © 1978 by Maya Angelou. Used by permission of Random House. An imprint and division of Penguin Random House LLC. All rights reserved.

Printed in the United States of America

*But his father said to the servants, "Quick! Bring the finest robe in
the house and put it on him. Get a ring for his finger and sandals for
his feet. And kill the calf we have been fattening. We must celebrate
with a feast, for this son of mine was dead and has now returned
to life. He was lost, but now he is found." So, the party began.*

—Luke 15:22–24 NLT

Contents

Acknowledgments vii

Introduction...xi

Chapter 1: Your Dominion in Life......................................1

Chapter 2: From Dominations into Abominations 8

Chapter 3: The Consequences of Losing Your Dominion 21

Chapter 4: Refuse to Live like a Loser 26

Chapter 5: Get to Your Senses..29

Chapter 6: I Will Rise..39

Chapter 7: Principle One: Remember................................45

Chapter 8: Principle Two: Repent....................................56

Chapter 9: Principle Three: Receive God's Grace and Glory.......70

Chapter 10: Principle Four: Make Restitution 77

Chapter 11: Principle Five: Renounce Your Past....................96

Chapter 12: Principle Six: Rejoice in the Lord 111

Chapter 13: Principle Seven: Repeat What God Had
Said about You 117

Chapter 14: Principle Eight: Reclaim Your Restoration
and Receive Your Revival.................................124

Chapter 15: Take Your Stand in the Lord............................132

Pray along with Me 151

ACKNOWLEDGMENTS

I surely have a lot of people to acknowledge and appreciate who believed in me and my dreams and have contributed immensely either directly or indirectly to my life and ministry. You have all been part of the story of my life. God bless you all real good.

To God, the Almighty, be all glory, honor, power, and praise.

I bless the name of the Lord for giving me the privilege to become a vessel that he uses to make an impact in life. I thank you, Lord Almighty, my all in all for giving me the vision, rousing the passion, making the provisions, granting the commission, and empowering the mission.

You are the beginner of all beginnings. You have no beginning, and you have no end. I cannot praise you enough and cannot stop praising you. Without You, I am nothing. I love you and will always love You, Jesus Christ my Savior, my Father, my God, my Lord, my King, and my Best Friend. You are indeed more than what people say.

To my beloved wife and the love of my life, Olasunbo Toyin Olorunnisola, my partner in ministry and a minister of God too, thank you for believing in me and for sharing my dreams, vision, future, and life with me. It is indeed true that "one will chase a thousand, but two will chase millions!" I love you always.

To my two lovely daughters, Sarah Oluwatise and Esther Oluwatamilore, I love you dearly.

I also dedicate this book to my family who all believe in me and my dreams and never give up on me.

To my lovely parents: Pastor Isaac and Evangelist Deborah Olorunnisola.

To my lovely siblings: Esther Sade, Victoria Lola, Ebenezer Tola, and Mary Lafe.

I love you all. God bless you all real good.

To illustrate the point further, Jesus told them this story: "A man had two sons. The younger son told his father, 'I want my share of your estate now before you die.' So, his father agreed to divide his wealth between his sons.

"A few days later this younger son packed all his belongings and moved to a distant land, and there he wasted all his money in wild living. About the time his money ran out, a great famine swept over the land, and he began to starve. He persuaded a local farmer to hire him, and the man sent him into his fields to feed the pigs. The young man became so hungry that even the pods he was feeding the pigs looked good to him. But no one gave him anything.

"When he finally came to his senses, he said to himself, 'At home, even the hired servants have food enough to spare, and here I am dying of hunger! I will go home to my father and say, "Father, I have sinned against both heaven and you, and I am no longer worthy of being called your son. Please take me on as a hired servant."'

"So, he returned home to his father. And while he was still a long way off, his father saw him coming. Filled with love and compassion, he ran to his son, embraced him, and kissed him. His son said to him, 'Father, I have sinned against both heaven and you, and I am no longer worthy of being called your son.'

"But his father said to the servants, 'Quick! Bring the finest robe in the house and put it on him. Get a ring for his finger and sandals for his feet. And kill the calf we have been fattening. We must celebrate with a feast, for this son of mine was dead and has now returned to life. He was lost, but now he is found.' So, the party began.

"Meanwhile, the older son was in the fields working. When he returned home, he heard music and dancing in the house, and he asked one of the servants what was going on. 'Your brother is back,' he was told, 'and your father has killed the fattened calf. We are celebrating because of his safe return.'

"The older brother was angry and wouldn't go in. His father came out and begged him, but he replied, 'All these years I've slaved for you and never once refused to do a single thing you told me to. And in all that time you never gave me even one young goat for a feast with my friends. Yet when this son of yours comes back after squandering your money on prostitutes, you celebrate by killing the fattened calf!'

"His father said to him, 'Look, dear son, you have always stayed by me, and everything I have is yours. We had to celebrate this happy day. For your brother was dead and has come back to life! He was lost, but now he is found!'" (Luke 15:11–32 NLT)

Introduction

A New Beginning

Jesus told the parable of the prodigal son in Luke 15:11–32 as a story that should always resonate in our minds whenever we think of reclaiming lost dominion. The younger son is our focus in this book. The younger son broke the hearts of everyone that loved him—his father, his brother, and the servants. He went far away from them—from his source—and wasted all his resources and inheritance on parties and prostitutes.

Later, a famine swept over the land. His money was all gone, and his newfound friends and lovers were all gone. He was left all alone. He was brokenhearted, lonely, depressed, abandoned, rejected, unforgiving, and unforgiven. His only means of survival was to tend to pigs—an abomination to his people. He not only lived with pigs but also ate the food given to pigs—a double-fold abomination.

He lived in abject poverty, humiliation, and hunger. Just like so many folks who had wasted God's resources and investment on them are living today, this young man wasted all the inheritance he got from his father. However, one day, he realized what he had lost. He then took some steps that I have outlined as the principles for a new beginning.

Finally, when he came to his senses, he remembered his purpose. He remembered where he was coming from. He knew he had a purpose. And he longed for the fulfillment of that purpose. This young man followed the eight principles for a new beginning, and he reclaimed his lost dominion.

The party began when he reclaimed his lost dominion. This book presents to you the eight principles for a new beginning to reclaim your lost dominion. As you apply these principles to your life, a new beginning will surely begin for you, and the world will celebrate your dominion. Get ready to celebrate your new beginning.

Jesus told this story so that we can also discover these principles. Applying these principles to your life would encourage and empower you to rise and recover your lost dominion.

Let the party begin!

CHAPTER 1

YOUR DOMINION IN LIFE

Dominion means sovereignty or control. It is also referred to as the territory of a sovereign or government. The kingdom is the territory of a king. The kingdom is the integration of two words—king and domain. Dominion also means ruling or controlling power, sovereign authority, a sphere of influence, and an area of control. When you oversee something or a rule, it also means the land that belongs to a ruler.

The parable made us understand that this young man was living in a place of dominion. The place of dominion is called a domain. Our character focus was the younger son of a wealthy man that had a very large estate and business empire.

He and his older brother were the only heirs to the wealth of their father. They either got equal shares or percentage difference, and being younger, he gets a lesser share. His father had many servants, and he has control over them as a son too. When you are in the place of your dominion, the following are bound to be adorned on you and to establish you as they did for this young man:

- Your garment
- Your dignity
- Your face
- Your voice

- Your inheritance
- Your honor
- Your name
- Your status
- Your authority

You have a dominion to occupy on earth. There is a place for you in history because there is a place for you in God.

> And God said, Let us make man in our image, after our likeness: and let them have dominion over the fish of the sea, and over the fowl of the air, and over the cattle, and over all the earth, and over all the creeping things that creepeth upon the earth. And God blessed them, and God said unto them, Be fruitful, and multiply, and replenish the earth, and subdue it: and have dominion over the fish of the sea, and over the fowl of the air, and over every living thing that moveth upon the earth. (Genesis 1:26, 28 KJV)

God created you to have dominion over all the earth. You are created for his glory. You are created for a purpose, and you must fulfill it.

> God spoke: "Let us make human beings in our image, make them reflection of our nature, So they can be responsible for the fish in the sea, the birds in the air, the cattle. And yes, the earth itself, and every animal that moves on the face of the earth…" God blessed them: "Prosper! Reproduce! Fill earth! Take charge! Be responsible for fish in the sea and birds in the air, for every living thing that moves on the face of earth." (The Message)

You reflect God's nature, and he created you to be responsible for all he has created.

> Then God said, "Let us make human beings in our image, to be like us. They will reign over the fish in the sea, the birds in the sky, the livestock, all the wild animals on the earth, and the small animals that scurry along the ground…" Then God blessed them and said, "Be fruitful and multiply. Fill the earth and govern it. Reign over the fish in the sea, the birds in the sky, and all the animals that scurry along the ground." (NLT)

You may not be born into any royalty or nobility, but you were born to reign. There is royalty in you. You belong to the kingdom of God.

> The God said, "Let us make mankind in Our image, according to our likeness, so they may rule over the fish of the sea and over the birds of the sky and over the livestock and over all the earth, and over every creeping thing that creeps on the earth…" God blessed them; and God said to them, "Be fruitful and multiply, and fill the earth, and subdue it; and rule over the fish of the sea and over the birds of the sky and over every living thing that moves on the earth." (NASB)

You are created to subdue and to rule over. God puts you in the domain for you to take dominion. The kingdom of God is in you.

> Then God said, Let us make man—someone like ourselves, to be master of all life upon the earth and in the skies and in the seas… And

God blessed them and told them, "Multiply and fill the earth and subdue it; you are masters of the fish and birds and all the animals." (TLB)

God calls you someone like Him. You share in the likeness of God. The likeness is not only in his image but also in his dominion.

The God said, "And now we will make human beings; they will be like us and resemble us. They will have power over the fish, the birds, and all animals, domestic and wild, large and small..." Blessed them, and said, "Have many children, so that your descendants will live all over the earth and bring it under their control. I am putting you in charge of the fish, the birds, and all the wild animals." (GNT)

There is a resemblance of God in you. And God has given you power over all he has created. He is also putting you in charge. You are responsible for where you are. That is your place of dominion.

Then God said, "Let us make humanity in our image to resemble us so that they may take charge of the fish of the sea, the birds in the sky, the livestock, all the earth, and all the crawling things on earth..." God blessed them and said to them, "Be fertile and multiply; fill the earth and master it. Take charge of the fish of the sea, the birds in the sky, and everything crawling on the ground." (CEB)

God created you to take charge. God puts you in charge to take charge. Dominion is your responsibility.

The God said, "Let Us (Father, Son, Holy Spirit) make man in Our image, according to

Our likeness (not physical, but a spiritual personality and moral likeness); and let them have complete authority over the fish of the sea, the birds of the air, the cattle, and over the entire earth, and over everything that creeps and crawls on the earth…" And God blessed them [granting them certain authority] and said to them, "Be fruitful and multiply, and fill the earth, and subjugate it (putting it under your power); and rule over (dominate) the fish of the sea, the birds of the air, and every living thing that moves upon the earth." (AMP)

You have been given the authority. It is left for you to discover it, uncover it, or recover it. Authority for dominion is in you, and you can only bring it out when you connect with the One who has given you that authority.

Look again at the words that were used in the passage from the various versions:

- Dominion
- Responsible for
- Reign over
- Master of
- Rule over
- Power
- Control
- Take charge
- Authority
- Subjugate

The heaven, even the heavens, are the Lord's: but the earth hath he given to the children of men. (Psalm 115:16)

The heavens are the heavens of the LORD.
But the earth He has give to the sons of mankind.
(NASB)

The heavens are the heavens of the LORD.
But the earth He has given to the children of
men. (AMP)

The LORD has kept the heavens for himself,
but he has given the earth to us humans. (CEV)

The heavens belong to the Lord, but he has
given the earth to all mankind. (TLB)

The heavens are the LORD's, but the earth
He has given to human race. (HCSB)

Heaven belongs to the LORD alone, but he
gave the earth to us humans. (GNT)

The heaven of heavens is for God, but he
put us in charge of the earth. (The Message)

The heavens belong to the LORD, but he has
given the earth to all humanity. (NLT)

You were created to take dominion on earth and fulfill the purpose of your creation. God has placed you where you are for a purpose. You will give an account of what you did on earth when you
get to heaven. Do not lose your place on earth. Take dominion, and
glorify God with it.

As we go further in this book, I want you to understand that
there is nothing wrong with you as a young man or young woman
leaving your parents' house to stay on your own. There is nothing
wrong with you leaving your parents' business empire to start your
own.

There is nothing wrong with you leaving your parents' church to start your own or join fellowship with another church. There is nothing wrong with you leaving your parents' city, hometown, or country for another place. Those are not what this book is all about.

You are meant for dominion. You are also meant to make an impact in your world.

CHAPTER 2

FROM DOMINATIONS INTO ABOMINATIONS

This young man, however, wanted a kingdom for himself. He wanted his own dominion. He wanted freedom. He asked for his inheritance and left the place of his dominion.

> The younger son told his father, "I want my share of your estate now before you die." So, his father agreed to divide his wealth between his sons. (Luke 15:12 NLT)

This young man left everything that had made his place of dominion a home worth living. He got himself some new friends and went far away from home.

> And not many days after the younger son gathered all together, and took his journey into a far country, and there wasted his substance with riotous living. (Luke 15:13)

> A few days later this younger son packed all his belongings and moved to a distant land,

and there he wasted all his money in wild living.
(Luke 15:13 NLT)

Your association will determine your direction and destination. Your association will determine your destination or your destitution. Your association will determine your decision and actions. In Nigeria, many have become victims of an evil incident called "one chance." Nigerians use public transportation a lot, and many evil and wicked people had taken advantage of that to rob and kidnap innocent passengers, sexually molest them, use them as ransom to demand money from their families, or kill them as rituals for wealth, power, and fame.

These evil people would park their cars or vans on the roadside and call out for a particular destination—local, long distance, and interstate—depending on the location. They operate at any time of the day and night. The driver or "bus conductor" would call the destination and add the tricky slogan "one chance." This means there is only one space left in the bus or car, and you are just the lucky person to get that seat.

Most of the time, all other passengers who are in the vehicle already are part of the evil plot, and you are just the victim. Sometimes, however, they use other innocent passengers as bait to get as much as they wanted. Many innocent lives had fallen prey to this evil act because people are always in a hurry to get to their destination. Some had failed to observe well the kind of people in the bus; some were just not sensitive enough because they were in a hurry.

The people would have thought it was their lucky day to have a bus going their way, and there was just one space left for them to get, and Nigerians are always in a hurry to get to whatever destination. The evil people would present it as a form of "help" they are rendering because Nigerians appreciate being helped.

These evil people took advantage of one of the two main desires of Nigerians:

- Always in a haste to get to somewhere or get things done fast
- Always appreciative and ready to receive an offer of help from someone else

I have heard from friends who had either fallen victims or knew those who had been victims. It is never a good ordeal to fall victim. Many never survived, many had gone missing forever, many never got to their destinations, many never returned to their families, many that survived had to live with the trauma for many years, and many never recovered from it.

That may be significant to Nigerians, but there are other issues of life that are significant to other nations and peoples, and the evil ones had taken advantage of them to get them into "one chance." It may not be nations this time, but it could be family issues, desires, and needs that the devil and evil ones had taken advantage of. The devil would want to entice you based on your current pressing needs.

> But every man is tempted, when he is drawn away of his own lust, and enticed. (James 1:14)

> But each one is tempted when he is dragged away, enticed and baited (to commit sin) by his own (worldly) desire (lust, passion). (AMP)

> Everyone is tempted by their own cravings; they are lured away and enticed by them. (CEB)

> No, a man's temptation is due to the pull of his own inward desires, which can be enormously attractive. (PHILLIPS)

> Temptation comes from our own desires, which entice us and drag us away. (NLT)

Let's look at some of those desires that the devil and wicked ones have used to lure many away from their domain of dominion and turn their dominations into abominations:

- Love
- Friendship

- Fame
- Family
- Companionship
- Help
- Satisfaction
- Fortunes

The list is endless because they are what we desire as humans, and they had become the bait for the devil and the wicked ones. What is that need of yours that has become the devil's bait too? There is only one that can satisfy your need, and he presents the remedy.

> Then Jesus said, "Come to me, all of you who are weary and carry heavy burdens, and I will give you rest. Take my yoke upon you. Let me teach you, because I am humble and gentle at heart, and you will find rest for your souls. For my yoke is easy to bear, and the burden I give you is light." (Matthew 11:28–30 NLT)

The "one chance" scenario is like the wild party the prodigal went for; he would have thought of getting it all fast. He would have thought of becoming famous faster than expected. He would have thought he was surrounded by friends who would applaud every one of his moves.

They were there to give him all the help he thought needed. He never knew he had fallen victim to a "one chance" party. Who have you associated with that has killed your dream? Who have you associated with that has killed something in you?

It is not everybody that is going in your direction and heading to the same destination with you that meant good for you. Many had become victims of the "one chance" party of life.

In life and in your quest to fulfill your destiny, you cannot share your dreams and desires with everybody or just anybody. Many of them are "one chance" to other people's destinies.

The friends went to the party with him. They pretended to offer help and did some favor but had only helped him to leave from domination to abomination and to waste all he had inherited. When he had wasted all he had and famine struck the land, no one of his party friends was there to at least encourage him. His party friends parted ways with him after they had helped him to waste all he had.

Who has offered you help only to kill your dreams and destiny? Who have you associated with that has killed your marriage, career, and business and ruined your life? Who have you associated your dream with? Who have you embarked with on the same journey of business, marriage, spiritual fellowship, and social?

The Prodigal Could Be a Victim Too

Let us delve into this issue from another perspective. Why would some young folks leave the place of dominion? Why would the young folks like to leave home and go far away from where they belong? Why would some young folks leave the church and leave the faith?

Some did not leave because they just wanted to be free nor because they were tempted or wrongly influenced to join the wild party. The influence came from outside because they could not see the influence for dominion on the inside. God is not happy with this, and he frowns at it:

> But whoso shall offend one of these little
> ones which believe in me, it were better for him
> that a millstone were hanged about his neck, and
> that he were drowned in the depth of the sea.
> Woe unto the world because of offences!
> for it must needs be that offences come; but
> woe to that man by whom the offence cometh!
> (Matthew 18:6–7)

It could be because of what they might have seen in the house. Jesus said that the father of the prodigal was a loving father, so he had no issue with his father. But there are many homes where love has been killed, and so the young folks found love elsewhere albeit the wrong kind of love.

Many have sought for the love they could not find in the house. Someone told them how beautiful they were. Someone told them how much they were loved. Someone told them how great they were endowed with their looks, body, and voice and how they can make a name, some fame, and fortunes with their endowment and had led them to join the wrong party of life.

> But if any of you causes one of these little ones who trusts in me to lose his faith, it would be better for you to have a rock tied to your neck and be thrown into the sea.
>
> Woe upon the world for all its evils. Temptation to do wrong is inevitable, but woe to the man who does the tempting. (Matthew 18:6–7 TLB)

Have you ever wondered why many millennials are leaving the church and never looking back at God? It could be that they left the church and the faith because they could not see the evidence of the faith in the lives of their parents. Listen again to what Jesus said:

> But whoever causes one of these little ones who believe in Me to stumble and sin (by leading him away from My teaching), it would be better for him to have a heavy millstone (as large as one turned by a donkey) hung around his neck and to be drowned in the depth of the sea.
>
> Woe (judgment is coming) to the world because of stumbling blocks and temptations to sin! It is inevitable that stumbling blocks come; but woe to the person on whose account or through whom the stumbling block comes! (Matthew 18:6–7 AMP)

It could be that they had lost trust in the church leadership too. There are many conflicts going on in the churches today. Those who were to be the shepherds have become the wolves. There are so many reports of abuse in the church: spiritual abuse, financial abuse, emotional abuse, physical abuse, sexual abuse.

These folks could not see the reason to trust in Jesus anymore because the church that was supposed to be the Body of Christ is full of abuses. And the spiritual leaders that were supposed to be the ambassadors of Christ were the ones doing the abuse. Many younger folks are bottling up many cases of abuse, and the people are covering it all up. They would have to take their leave when they could no longer bottle up such things.

> But if anyone abuses one of these little ones who believes in me, it would be better for him to have a heavy boulder tied around his neck and be hurled into the deepest sea than to face the punishment he deserves!
>
> Misery will come to the one who lures people away into sin. Troubles and obstacles to your faith are inevitable, but great devastation will come to the one guilty of causing others to stumble! (Matthew 18:6–7 The Passion Translation)

Some had left their denominations for some sort of fellowship that has occult motives. Some had been indoctrinated with some mindset against faith and church leadership that they would always question what the Bible says. Some had been made to believe that the Bible is just another book of history.

Some had preferred to stay far away from the church and church people. Only a few of them had found better places and better churches to go. The others have become prey for the devil to further take advantage of and further destroy.

> But if you give them a hard time, bullying or taking advantage of their simple trust,

you'll soon wish you hadn't. You'd be better off dropped in the middle of the lake with a millstone around your neck. Doom to the world for giving these God-believing children a hard time! Hard times are inevitable, but you don't have to make it worse—and it's doomsday to you if you do. (Matthew 18:6–7 The Message)

The saddest part is that as many are being made victims, they are also influencing others to become potential victims too, and the trend is ongoing.

Jesus said this unequivocally:

The thief's purpose is to steal and kill and destroy. My purpose is to give life in all its fullness. (John 10:10 NLT)

Your life and destiny are seeds in the hands of God. The devil (the thief) never meant any good for you. He has come to steal from you, to contend it with you, and to offer you what is fake to take away the original from you. He has come to kill your destiny. He has come to destroy you before you grow up to realize what your life is all about.

Jesus, however, had said that his purpose is that you might have life in all its fullness. "In all its fullness" means you will grow to fulfill what God has created you for. "In all its fullness" means that you have a purpose to fulfill in life. "In all its fullness" means you have a place of dominion. "In all its fullness" means if only you abide in him and he lives in you, you will enjoy life in its fullness. "In all its fullness" means there is a party that seems good for you because all other young folks are enjoying it, but it is the way of death.

There is a way that seems right to a man, But its end is the way of death. (Proverbs 16:25 NKJV)

> There is a way which seems right to a man
> and appears straight before him, But its end is the
> way of death. (AMP)

> Before every man there lies a wide and
> pleasant road he thinks is right, but it ends in
> death. (TLB)

> What you think is the right road may lead
> to death. (GNT)

> There is a path before each person that
> seems right, but it ends in death. (NLT)

"In all its fullness" means God has prepared a party for you waiting for you to come back home. The party will not begin until you return to where you belong.

> Jesus told him, "I am the way, the truth, and
> the life. No one can come to the Father except
> through me." (John 8:32 NLT)

> Jesus said to him, "I am the (only) Way (to
> God) and the (real) Truth and the (real) Life; no
> one comes to the Father but through Me." (AMP)

These young folks, however, have been offended by the attitudes of their parents and the spiritual leaders. These attitudes had led the younger folks far away from the dominion God had made them for.

They looked for the ways that others are going. They looked for the ways of the people that made them feel good too. They thought that the other ways would appreciate their self-worth outside of

Christ but never knew the devil had worse plans for them. They had gone from domination to abomination.

> But if you cause one of these little ones who trusts in me to fall into sin, it would be better for you to have a large millstone tied around your neck and be drowned in the depths of the sea.
> What sorrow awaits the world because it tempts people to sin. Temptations are inevitable, but what sorrow awaits the person who does the tempting. (Matthew 18:6–7 NLT)

The young man associated with the wrong friends, and they went for the wrong party. The wrong party of life could mean wrong lifestyle that is outside of the will of God for your life. They may include but are not limited to the following:

- Wrong lifestyle
- Wrong fellowship
- Wrong music
- Wrong friends
- Wrong ideology of life
- Wrong books and literature
- Wrong opinions
- Wrong influence on social media
- Wrong attitude to life
- Wrong views on marriage
- Wrong ways to dress, redress, and be addressed

They partied all day and all night, and it was as if they were having the best time of their lives until they had wasted all he had inherited. The younger son broke the hearts of everyone that loved him—his father, his brother, and the servants.

He went far away from them—from his source—and wasted all his resources and inheritance on parties and prostitutes. Many had wasted their talents, dreams, and lives going for the wrong party of life.

> About the time his money ran out, a great famine swept over the land, and he began to starve. (Luke 15:14 NLT)

Later, a famine swept over the land. His money was all gone, and his newfound friends and lovers were all gone. He was left all alone. He was brokenhearted, lonely, depressed, abandoned, rejected, unforgiving, and unforgiven. The sad part was that after he had wasted all his resources and inheritance, those who had gone partying with him parted ways with him. He was left all alone and had no means of survival.

Such is life—when you have it all to blow off, people will gather around you, but after you have blown it all off, people will leave you, and you will be left alone to gather the pieces of your blown life, that is, if you have any piece left.

So why would you go for the wrong party of life? However, you can still get a new lease of life and get back to where you belong. The principles for a new beginning are there to guide your steps.

> He persuaded a local farmer to hire him, and the man sent him into his fields to feed the pigs. The young man became so hungry that even the pods he was feeding the pigs looked good to him. But no one gave him anything. (Luke 15:15–16 NLT)

His only means of survival was to tend to pigs—an abomination to his people. He not only lived with pigs but also ate the food given to pigs—a double-fold abomination. He lived in abject poverty, humiliation, and hunger. Just like so many folks who had wasted God's resources and investment on them are living today, they live from domination to abomination.

These are also signs of the end of times. We are in dangerous times, and it is getting more difficult to be living as Christians. The Bible had warned that many Christians will be lured out of the dominion. The culture of these present times will make it difficult for Christians. God has forewarned, so there is a remedy.

> You should know this, Timothy, that in the last days there will be very difficult times. For people will love only themselves and their money. They will be boastful and proud, scoffing at God, disobedient to their parents, and ungrateful. They will consider nothing sacred. They will be unloving and unforgiving; they will slander others and have no self-control. They will be cruel and hate what is good. They will betray their friends, be reckless, be puffed up with pride, and love pleasure rather than God. They will act religious, but they will reject the power that could make them godly. Stay away from people like that! (2 Timothy 3:1–5 NLT)

> But you must realize that in the last days the times will be full of danger. Men will become utterly self-centered, greedy for money, full of big words. They will be proud and contemptuous, without any regard for what their parents taught them. They will be utterly lacking in gratitude, purity, and normal human affections. They will be men of unscrupulous speech and have no control of themselves. They will be passionate and unprincipled, treacherous, self-willed, and conceited, loving all the time what gives them pleasure instead of loving God. They will maintain a facade of "religion," but their conduct will deny its validity. You must keep clear of people like this. (PHILLIPS)

Don't be naive. There are difficult times ahead. As the end approaches, people are going to be self-absorbed, money-hungry, self-promoting, stuck-up, profane, contemptuous of parents, crude, coarse, dog-eat-dog, unbending, slanderers, impulsively wild, savage, cynical, treacherous, ruthless, bloated windbags, addicted to lust, and allergic to God. They'll make a show of religion, but behind the scenes they're animals. Stay clear of these people. (The Message)

CHAPTER 3

THE CONSEQUENCES OF LOSING YOUR DOMINION

When you lose your dominion, you burn inside with anger and bitterness. And these may express themselves in a number of ways. It affects you either as a prey for the wrong party or as a part of the wrong party as you fail to look unto God for the necessary healing and solution but turn somewhere else or to someone else for the healing.

> He persuaded a local farmer to hire him,
> and the man sent him into his fields to feed the
> pigs. (Luke 15:15 NLT)

King David wrote in the Psalms to describe how his guilt had affected him.

> There was a time when I wouldn't admit
> what a sinner I was. But my dishonesty made me
> miserable and filled my days with frustration. All
> day and all night your hand was heavy on me.
> My strength evaporated like water on a sunny
> day until I finally admitted all my sins to you and

stopped trying to hide them. I said to myself, "I
will confess them to the Lord." And you forgave
me! All my guilt is gone. (Psalm 32:3–5 TLB)

Apart from guilt, bitterness also takes a toll on those who have
lost their dominion and have fallen from domination to abomination. Let us look at some of the ways we are being affected by taking
a closer look at this young man that was left alone to his fate.

I will like you to look at this from two perspectives—one, the
dominion you lost because of your actions and decision, and two, the
dominion you lost because of you falling prey to the mistakes or evil
acts of others:

- Physical
- Emotional
- Spiritual
- Relational

Physical

Losing dominion may lead to unresolved guilt and bitterness,
which may affect us physically. This usually manifests in various
ways: imagined sickness, headaches, stomach disorders, exhaustion,
vague pains, and even some real illness.

If we try to run from our guilt and pains by immersing ourselves
in work or covering it up in one way or the other, we will pay a price.
Eventually, our bodies will take a toll on us. He became unkempt and
unhealthy. Imagine the young man that was adorned with beautiful
clothes now dressed in rags.

Emotional

Psychologists and counselors have confirmed the following as
emotional effects of offending and being offended: depression, anger,
self-pity, feelings of inadequacy, denial of responsibility. The young

man lost all his inheritance and was left all alone. He was filled with anger and self-pity and was depressed.

Spiritual

Unresolved guilt, pains, and bitterness may have the following spiritual effects on us: a sense of alienation from God, inability to pray. He could no longer call upon his God again. Loss of dominion led him to commit an abomination. He not only worked to raise pigs but also ate the food meant for the pigs.

He could not think of prayers but only ponder on the guilt and pains he was passing through. He could not think of prayers but the anger and bitterness he was experiencing. He complained that he had no man to help him. His friend had left him. He could not go to the synagogue to pray.

Reduced fellowship with believers and inability to read the Bible also take a toll on us. And there will no longer be a feeling of joy, just like the man had experienced. That is the case with many today who had allowed guilt and bitterness to have a place in their lives. Some unresolved anger and bitterness also go a long way to block your prayers from being answered and even affect your spiritual life and growth, likewise, some unresolved, unpardoned, and unforgiven offenses.

Relational

This young man said to himself, "I have no one. I am alone and lonely." Losing dominion will have an impact on our relationships with others in various ways, like blaming ourselves and others for our predicament, irritation, profuse apologies, withdrawal, loneliness, self-justification, refusal to accept compliments, and outburst of temper.

Likewise, some of us have had major parts of our lives affected by the hurt, offense, and shame that people had caused us or had put us into. These would touch us physically, emotionally, spiritually, and relationally. But if we can cry out to God and find forgiveness in him, we will be able to enjoy our lives again.

Jesus, however, promises you a new beginning. And he is calling you to come to him.

> Then Jesus said, "Come to me, all of you who are weary and carry heavy burdens, and I will give you rest. Take my yoke upon you. Let me teach you, because I am humble and gentle at heart, and you will find rest for your souls. For my yoke is easy to bear, and the burden I give you is light." (Matthew 11:28–30 NLT)

> *Wouldst thou, O weary soul, be blest?*
> *In Christ the Lord thy Saviour see;*
> *His Grace alone can give thee rest,*
> *And lo! He calleth, "Come to Me!"*
>
> *Oh, come to Me! Oh, come to Me!*
> *The Saviour calleth, "Come to Me,"*
> *Ye heavy laden, come to Me,*
> *And I will give you rest.*
>
> *He does not wait for greater worth,*
> *Or more of holiness in thee;*
> *He brings good news to all the earth,*
> *And still He calleth, "Come to Me!"*
>
> *Hast thou not sinned ten thousand times?*
> *His pardoning grace will set thee free;*
> *Count unbelief the worst of crimes,*
> *And trust thy Saviour's, "Come to Me!"*

Eternal life is in His word,
He asks thee now His child to be;
No sweeter sound was ever heard,
Than His most gracious, "Come to Me!"

Be this thine answer now and here,
"Since thou hast kindly called for me;
Thy tender love dispels my fear,
I come, I come, O Lord, to Thee!"

—Rev. J Clark

However, the poor man is not he who has no penny, but he who had no purpose.

CHAPTER 4

REFUSE TO LIVE LIKE A LOSER

Every sin has a past. Every sinner has a future.

You must stop looking for sympathy and start looking for a solution. You must stop looking back to reflect on what you have done to others or what others have done to you. You must begin to face the reality. Stop looking over your shoulder.

You don't get recognition and sympathy by letting people see you as the victim or the loser; you get it by letting people see you as the victor who has overcome being a victim. The world never celebrates victims. They sympathize with them.

How long will you live in sympathy for men to get attention? The world celebrates victors, not victims. You should understand the difference between celebration and sympathy. This young man begged for a humiliating job, yet no one looked at him. He begged for food, yet no one looked at him. He struggled to eat the food meant for pigs, yet no one looked at him.

He persuaded a local farmer to hire him, and
the man sent him into his fields to feed the pigs.
The young man became so hungry that even the
pods he was feeding the pigs looked good to him.

> But no one gave him anything. (Luke 15:15–16 NLT)

The local farmer could have pitied him because he was the young man that threw the wild party a few times ago. But no, he could only get the pity that made the farmer give him the job, not even food. Being a victim does not attract attention for dominion but of humiliation. The young man got to his senses and said to himself, "I will arise."

The tentacles of yesterday's tragedies are most times longer than our hope. This is because they've gotten inside of us—sometimes real deep inside—that we find it difficult to hope for a new and better beginning. But you must try as you might to outrun that yesterday's tragedies.

If you were at fault, it would be different. If you were to blame, you could apologize. But you weren't the culprit. You were a victim. You were terrorized, molested, brutalized, abused, robbed, falsely accused, disappointed, jilted, cheated on, abandoned, rejected. And that bitterness, shame, and pain are rooting deeper and growing taller inside of you.

Sometimes, your shame is private. No one else knows. But only you know. You carry it all alone—for years. And that's enough. Sometimes, it is public. Everybody else knows. And everyone has his own version of your predicament.

Whether private or public, shame is always painful. Unless you deal with it, it is going to be permanent. Unless you cry for help, you will never get help. Unless you get help, you will continue to grope in the darkness and the light will never come. You must get over that shame. You must start longing for victory and stop living like a victim.

God said, "I have set before you an open door which no man can shut" (Revelations 3:8). However, you must shut the door to your past before you can walk through the door to your future. *Until a door closes, another cannot be opened.* God has opened the door for you, but he wants us to walk through them and accept responsibility for your future.

Finally, he came to his senses and remembered his purpose. He remembered where he was coming from. He knew he had a purpose. And he longed for it. This young man followed the eight principles for a new beginning, and he reclaimed his lost dominion.

The party began when he reclaimed his lost dominion. I want to present to you the eight principles for a new beginning to reclaim your lost dominion. As you apply these principles to your life, a new beginning will surely begin for you, and the world will celebrate your dominion. Get ready to celebrate your new beginning.

Let the party begin!

CHAPTER 5

GET TO YOUR SENSES

And when he came to himself, he said, How many hired servants of my father's have bread enough and to spare, and I perish with hunger! (Luke 15:17)

But when he (finally) came to his senses, he said, "How many of my father's hired men have more than enough food, while I am dying here of hunger!" (AMP)

When he finally came to his senses, he said to himself, "At home even the hired men have food enough and to spare, and here I am, dying of hunger!" (TLB)

But when he came to his senses, he said, "How many of my father's hired laborers have more than enough bread, but I am dying here from hunger!" (NASB)

To reclaim your lost dominion, you will need to get to your senses. That was what Isaac told Esau when Jacob stole his blessings. The blessings had been transferred long before the stealing. Esau had sold his birthright for a plate of food because of a wrong orientation about life and destiny.

> One day when Jacob was cooking some stew, Esau arrived home from the wilderness exhausted and hungry. Esau said to Jacob, "I'm starved! Give me some of your stew!" (This is how Esau got his other name, Edom, which means "red.").
> "All right," Jacob replied, "but traded me your rights as the firstborn son."
> "Look, I'm dying of starvation!" said Esau. "What good is my birthright now?"
> But Jacob said, "First you must swear that your birthright is mine." So Esau swore an oath, thereby selling all his rights as the firstborn to his brother, Jacob. Then Jacob gave Esau some bread and lentil stew. Esau ate the meal, then got up and left. He showed contempt for his rights as the firstborn. (Genesis 25:29–4 NLT)

Many could not understand who they are and had sold out their rights to others. Just to satisfy an immediate hunger, Esau lost his destiny. What have you sold out to satisfy an immediate urge or solution? What rights have you sold out because you wanted to satisfy an immediate need? It could be your birthright, your copyright, even your freedom right, right to live, and right to life.

> In the words of the Scriptures, "I loved Jacob, but I rejected Esau." (Romans 9:13)

> Make sure that no one is immoral or godless like Esau, who traded his birthright as the firstborn son for a single meal. (Hebrews 12:16 NLT)

God is always angry at those who sell their identities because they had a wrong orientation about their lives and destinies. A wrong orientation is a wild party of life. The "one chance" agents are always there to prey on your soul and destroy your life.

These evil forces will always surround you to take dominion over your life. They can be anything—the social media, your ungodly friends, wrong books, and, sadly, some religious fathers. Yes, I mean, some pastors can be agents on the wild party of life that steals and destroys potentials in their members and their destinies.

Your Dimensions of Senses

> When he finally came to his senses, he said to himself, "At home, even the hired servants have food enough to spare, and here I am dying of hunger! I will go home to my father and say, 'Father, I have sinned against both heaven and you, and I am no longer worthy of being called your son. Please take me on as a hired servant.'"
> (Luke 15:17–19 NLT)

Since the enemy doesn't want you to know you have authority over him, he uses his strategies to keep you down and out. He attacks your heart (your emotions and willpower). He uses all your sense organs and transmits the impulse to your heart. Just as your biological heart works, so is your spiritual heart. That is why the Bible always charges us to "gird our hearts with all diligence for out of it comes the issue of life."

> Keep thy heart with all diligence, for out of it are the issues of life. Put away from thee a forward mouth, and perverse lips put far from thee. Ponder the path of thy feet and let all thy ways be established. Turn not to the right hand nor to the left: remove thy foot from evil. (Proverbs 4:23–27)

Let's consider the three dimensions of senses the enemy uses to make you not to reclaim your dominion:

- Your sense of feelings
- Your sense of perception
- Your sense of proclamation

Your Sense of Feelings

This includes your sense of smell, sense of hearing, and, majorly, sense of touch—the skin. The skin covers all parts of your body, so you feel the touch everywhere. These feelings have to do with your reasoning and emotions.

Since the devil doesn't give up territory without a fight, expect to be tested on this so as not to be caught off guard. Time and time again, he will come back and offer you the same old issues, all wrapped up in the skin of reason and emotions, just like how your physical skin reacts to weathering conditions.

For example, it was winter, and you were cold and almost frozen to death. Then a fireplace was prepared for you, and you were brought there to get warm. Still, time and time again, you remember that terrifying moment you had in the freezing cold outside. And that moment would make you still feel cold despite being near a fireplace.

If you let it get to your mindset, you may be warmed up yet still feel cold. *This is when you need to develop a thick skin against your pains and your past.* Do not let it get to your skin.

Another example is this: you were almost choked up by some fumes. Then you were rescued and brought to a clean area. Time and time again, the feeling of those horrible fumes would come to you. And when it gets to your mindset, you might be breathing very clean air yet still perceive the deadly fumes.

It's all in your feelings. And it's through your reasoning and emotions.

The devil tells you, "You don't feel like you're free. It's still coming back to you." He tells you, "You don't feel forgiven. Who can ever forgive you for such awful actions?" He tells you, "Can you really forgive and forget such? Just remember and see that you can never forget because it will always come back to you!" He asks you, "Are you sure you have totally gotten over it? Can't you feel it coming back to you?"

The devil uses your feelings to still hold you bound to your past. It is for you to stand your ground and claim what has been done on your behalf. That is where your victory is decided. With all diligence, you gird your feelings—your sense of emotions.

The work of victory has been done for you and in you. All you need to do is to rise to a new beginning. God has declared you free. His Word had said so. His blood has done the work. His name had confirmed it. And you must begin to live it too.

Satan would want to bring back to your mind the things God has set you free from. He wants to make you feel that nothing has changed. He wants to make you feel that the past will always come back. He wants to make you feel that you will have to fight it again. He wants to make you feel that victory is not totally guaranteed for you.

But you must be single-minded in your stand, and as Paul declared, "I am bringing all my energies to bear on this one thing: Forgetting the past and looking forward to what lies ahead" (Philippians 3:13 TLB).

Your Sense of Perception

This has to do with your sense of sight—your eyes, also your sense of taste—especially the aftertaste effect. The devil will make you see the same battle and the same trouble around you. He will make you see many other victims having the same or similar past experiences. He will make you see that you are not the only victim—and tell you to join the pity party.

He will make you see that no progress is made since you have been fighting that battle. He will make you see despair and disappointment in everything you do. He will make you see the wounds—that it cannot be healed because it still looks fresh. He will make you see the scars—as a permanent reminder because they cannot be covered. He will make you see people mocking you and making jest of you. He will make you see people who want to help you as potential culprits who would break your heart again.

That was the case of the man that went blind. He wasn't born blind, but something happened somewhere, sometime, somehow, and maybe through someone. But when he met with Jesus, Jesus touched his eyes.

> Jesus took the blind man by the hand and led him out of the village, and spat upon his eyes, and laid his hands over them. "Can you see anything now?" Jesus asked him.
>
> The man looked around "Yes!" he said, "I see men! But I can't see them clearly: they look like tree trunks walking around!"
>
> Then Jesus placed his hands over the man's eyes again and as the man stared intently, his sight was completely restored, and he saw everything clearly, drinking in the sights around him. (Mark 8:23–25 TLB)

Jesus had to touch him again for the man's sight to be fully restored. He saw men walking like trees. But Jesus gave him the second touch. All you also need is another touch from Jesus. Let him touch you again. You will see clearly what God wants you to see and not the picture the devil would want to bring to you.

Your Sense of Proclamation

This has to do with your tongue and mouth. The devil wants you to speak negatively to yourself. Firstly, he would make you feel negative. Secondly, he would make you see the negative. Thirdly, he would make you speak the negative. Finally, he would make you always live in the negative that you have felt, seen, and spoken of.

The devil will want to make you feel you are a victim, see yourself as a victim, declare yourself as a victim, and then live all your life as a victim. Sadly, many have fallen, and many are falling victims of this victimizing strategy of the devil, all in the name of seeking comfort. The young man declared to himself the following:

> At home, even the hired servants have food enough to spare, and here I am dying of hunger! I will go home to my father and say, "Father, I have sinned against both heaven and you, and I am no longer worthy of being called your son. Please take me on as a hired servant." (Luke 15:18 NLT)

He said, "I will arise and go back to reclaim my dominion." *Words are very powerful. What you say to yourself will go a long way to affect your life.*

> You are snared with the words of your lips;
> you are caught in the speech of your mouth.
> (Proverbs 6:2 AMP)

> You may have trapped yourself by your agreement. (Proverbs 6:2 TLB)

The tongue may be delicate, but it is the most powerful sense organ in the body. That is why it is advisable to guard your words, for they create the atmosphere you live in. You must never say things that make the enemy think he's winning and you are losing. You are a victor and not a victim. And as you rise, you must speak positively to yourself.

> If anyone can control his tongue, it proves that he has perfect control over himself in every other way. We can make a large horse turn around and go wherever we want by means of a small bit in his mouth. And a tiny rudder makes a huge ship turn wherever the pilot wants it to go, even though the winds are strong.

So also, the tongue is a small thing, but what enormous damage it can do.

A great forest can be set on fire by one tiny spark. And the tongue is a flame of fire. It is full of wickedness and poisons every part of the body. And the tongue is set on fire by hell itself and can turn our whole lives into a blazing fire of destruction and disaster.

Men have trained or can train, every kind of animal or bird that lives and every kind of reptile and fish, but no human being can tame the tongue. It is always ready to pour out its deadly poison. Sometimes it praises our heavenly Father, and sometimes it breaks out into curses against men who are made like God. And so, blessing and cursing come pouring out of the same mouth. Dear brothers, surely this is not right! (James 3:2–10 TLB)

Self-control means controlling the tongue! A quick retort can ruin everything! (Proverbs 13:3 TLB)

Anxious hearts are very heavy, but a word of encouragement does wonders! (Proverbs 12:25 TLB)

From a wise mind comes careful and persuasive speech. Kind words are like honey—enjoyable and healthful. (Proverbs 16:23–24 TLB)

You must not let the devil use your speech to bring you down. Always speak positively to yourself. You are a success, not a failure. You will make it. You are a victor and not a victim.

Who are you? How do you define yourself? Are you easily sold out to satisfy your needs? It is sad to say that many had sold out their soul to the devil to get fame and fortunes. To God, they are already dead even when they are still alive and enjoying the moment.

Do not let the wild party prey on you and take away your dreams and destiny and terminate your life in the land far away. Get back to your senses. That was what Isaac told Esau.

> Finally, his father, Isaac, said to him, "You will live away from the richness of the earth, and away from the dew of the heaven above. You will live by your sword, and you will serve your brother. But when you decide to break free, you will shake his yoke from your neck." (Genesis 27:39–40 NLT)

The King James Version says, "When you shall have dominion, that you shall break his yoke from off your neck." The Message Version says, "When you can't take it anymore, you'll break loose and run free." New International Version says, "When you grow restless, you will throw his yoke from off your neck." Good News Translation says, "Yet when you rebel, you will break away from his control." New American Standard Bible says, "But it shall come to about when you become restless, that you will break his yoke from your neck."

All these narrow down the statement "When you get to your senses." "When you realize your identity."

When Esau got his senses back, Jacob was even scared of him. Read about their reconciliation in Genesis 33.

> When he finally came to his senses, he said to himself, "At home, even the hired servants have food enough to spare, and here I am dying of hunger! I will go home to my father and say, 'Father, I have sinned against both heaven and you, and I am no longer worthy of being called your son. Please take me on as a hired servant.'" (Luke 15:17–19 NLT)

On getting to your senses, you will realize you have been carrying the wrong orientation—either you have allowed it or you have inherited it. On getting to your senses, you will realize that you have been enslaved and used for a long time, and then you will regain your freedom. On getting to your senses, you will change the way you see yourself. On getting to your senses, you will realize that you need to get out of the wayside of life. On getting to your senses, you will pour your anger on your anguish and take back the dominion of your life.

CHAPTER 6

I WILL RISE

> I will arise and go to my father, and will say unto him, Father, I have sinned against heaven, and before thee, And am no more worthy to be called thy son: make me as one of thy hired servants.
>
> And he arose and came to his father. But when he was yet a great way off, his father saw him, and had compassion, and ran, and fell on his neck, and kissed him. (Luke 15:18–20)

Arise here is an action word. Once you get your senses to "arise," it is your responsibility to act and "arise."

If you are sick and you are tired of being sick, then you are ready to get healed.

Rising from where one has fallen is not easy though. If it was, everybody would be doing it. But each time you fall, God wants you to rise and get up on your feet again. He doesn't want you to live in your past; he wants you to live for the future.

No matter how hard you have fallen, God wants you to rise. No matter how bad you have fallen, God wants you to rise. No matter how terrible you have fallen, God wants you to rise. No matter how horrible you have fallen, God wants you to rise. No matter how painful you have fallen, God wants you to rise. No matter how shameful you have fallen, God wants you to rise.

It is in your rising that you get your healing and not in your sitting or lying down there.

Medical doctors do not confirm a patient is totally healed until they see him rise on his feet. So is God. *He leads you on the pathway to reclaiming your dominion with your rising.*

Let's see what the Bible has to say about your rising:

> As for me, I look to the Lord for my help; I wait for God to save me; He will hear me. Do not rejoice against me; O my enemy, for though I fall, I will rise again! When I sit in darkness, the Lord himself will be my light. (Micah 7:7–8 TLB)

When you fall, you will rise again. God is there to shine his light into your darkness. And he is still stretching out his hand to lift you up from where you have fallen.

> The steps of good men are directed by the Lord. He delights in each step they take. If they fall, it isn't fatal, for the Lord holds them with His hand. (Psalms 37:23–24 TLB)

Though you fall, it isn't fatal. Your falling is not the end of your life. It is not the conclusion of the matter. God will turn that pain into a gain for you. And he will turn those scars into stars.

> O evil man, leave the upright man alone and quit trying to cheat him out of his rights. Don't you know that this good man, though you trip him seven times, will each time rise again? But one calamity is enough to lay you down. (Proverb 24:15–16 TLB)

Though you may fall seven times, each time, God will lift you up. Though people may make you a victim seven times, each time, you will rise a victor. You must not let one calamity lay you down and knock you out. Rise up, and live again.

However, let me also add a warning here, especially when somebody who offends you or had made you a victim falls into calamity.

> Do not rejoice when your enemy meets trouble. Let there no be gladness when he falls—for the Lord may be displeased with you and stop pushing him! (Proverbs 24:17–18 TLB)

> The Lord supports the humble but brings the wicked into the dust. (Proverbs 147:6 TLB)

> The good man does not escape all troubles—he has them too. But the Lord helps him in each and every one. Not one of his bones is broken. (Psalm 34:19–20 TLB)

We cannot escape all troubles. We all have our pasts. Most times, they are ugly. But these pasts are not determinants of our future, and they must not be. All we need to do is to obey the commands of God and *rise*.

> *Each step I take my Savior goes before me*
> *And with His loving hand He leads the way*
> *And with each breath I whisper "I adore Thee;"*
> *Oh, what joy to walk with him each day.*
>
> *Each step I take I know that He will guide me;*
> *To higher ground He ever leads me on.*
> *Until I some day the last step will be taken*
> *Each step I take just leads me closer home.*

At time I feel my faith begin to waver,
When up ahead I see a chasm wide,
It's then I turn and look up to my Savior,
I am strong when He is by my side.

I trust in God, no matter come what may,
For life eternal is in His hand,
He holds the key that opens up the way
That will lead me to the Promised Land.

—W. Elmo Merce

Eight Principles for a New Beginning

Let me reveal to you some eight principles to take as you rise to reclaim your lost dominion. *In your rising, you are revived. In the spiritual realm, the number eight stands for a new beginning.*

This means after every work is done, completed, and perfected by the number seven, the next step is to *start a new beginning*. And the number eight stands for that. Your rising up is your responsibility. Every step you take is your responsibility.

There is always a comeback for every setback. You might have encountered setbacks because of being the offender or the offended, but when God tells you to rise to a new beginning, there is a comeback. And your comeback will always be greater and more glorious than your setback. The young man said, "I will arise!" His proclamation led to his reclamation. Proclaim it to reclaim it. Tell yourself, "I (put your name) will arise!"

Declare this to yourself: "Though I have setbacks, I have a comeback, and I will take the steps for my comeback. My comeback is greater and more glorious than my setback. My comeback and rising to a new beginning are my responsibility, and I am taking those steps now. So help me, God. Amen."

I felt inspired as I read the poem written by Maya Angelou titled "I Rise." This poem could inspire you too. Say to yourself, "I will rise."

You may write me down in history
With your bitter, twisted lies,
You may trod me in the very dirt
But still, like dust, I'll rise.

Does my sassiness upset you?
Why are you beset with gloom?
'Cause I walk like I've got oil wells
Pumping in my living room.

Just like moons and like suns,
With the certainty of tides,
Just like hopes springing high,
Still I'll rise.

Did you want to see me broken?
Bowed head and lowered eyes?
Shoulders falling down like teardrops,
Weakened by my soulful cries?

Does my haughtiness offend you?
Don't you take it awful hard
'Cause I laugh like I've got gold mines
Diggin' in my own backyard.

You may shoot me with your words,
You may cut me with your eyes,
You may kill me with your hatefulness,
But still, like air, I'll rise.

Does my sexiness upset you?
Does it come as a surprise
That I dance like I've got diamonds
At the meeting of my thighs?

Out of the huts of history's shame
I rise
Up from a past that's rooted in pain
I rise
I'm a black ocean, leaping and wide,
Welling and swelling I bear in the tide.

Leaving behind nights of terror and fear
I rise
Into a daybreak that's wondrously clear
I rise
Bringing the gifts that my ancestors gave,
I am the dream and the hope of the slave.
I rise
I rise
I rise.

CHAPTER 7

PRINCIPLE ONE: REMEMBER

He *remembered* his first love with his father.

> When he finally came to his senses, he said
> to himself, "At home, even the hired men have
> food enough and to spare, and here I am, dying
> of hunger!" (Luke 15:17 TLB)

When he came to his senses, something triggered in his memory. He could remember. This is the first principle that leads to a new beginning. It is the first step you take as you rise to recover your lost dominion. Remember. There are some pasts worth forgetting, and there are some pasts worth remembering.

The pasts worth remembering are those pasts you had with God. Those beautiful moments you had before you fell out of grace, before you lost your dominion, and before you fell victim. I am talking to Christians now. Remember the times you gave your life to Jesus. Remember the times you said, "I surrender all." Remember your first love.

> Nevertheless, I have this against you, that
> you have left your first love. Remember therefore
> where you have fallen… (Revelation 2:4–5a)

> Yet there is one thing wrong; you don't love
> me as at first! Think about those times of your
> first love (how different now!)... (Revelation
> 2:4–5a TLB)

If there is no tendency to forget, there won't be any reason to remember. God knows we have the tendency to forget, so he charged us to remember our first love. To remember is the first step needed in your rising up to a new life. You cannot skip this first principle. It is a step worth taking. It leads to greater heights and opens all other doors.

When he got to his senses, he could remember. If you cannot remember, you cannot recover. If you cannot recollect, you cannot reconnect.

You recollect those times you had with Christ, those times before you fell victim, and those times before you lost your dominion. The young man recalled those times when he was in his father's house.

He remembered the talks he used to have with his father. He remembered walks he used to have with his father. He remembered doing chores and running errands with his brother. He remembered giving orders to his servants.

God is significantly interested in your past, present, and future. I am not sounding contradictory to what I would say later on forgetting your past. That haunting past needs to be forgotten. However, the past God is referring to here are the moments you once shared with him.

Remember those moments of prayer, those moments of praise, those moments of studying the Bible. Remember those moments of fellowship you had with other Christians. Remember those moments of telling somebody about Jesus, those moments of sharing your testimonies with everyone who could hear.

Remember those moments of joy and peace. God wants you to think about those moments. Recall how great it once was, not how bad it has become. Recall the best of times, not the worst of it.

There is something that would always trigger you to remember. This young man was living in the exact opposite of his life when he had dominion. Then he came to his senses. Let's look at those things that made him remember where he needed to be and who he needed to become:

- He was now tending to swine, which was an abomination. He remembered his domination and how servants attend to him.
- He was now rearing swine, which was an abomination. He remembered the numbers of sheep and cattle his father has, which gave them domination in the land.
- He was now eating the food meant for pigs. He remembered eating at a wealthy and clean table in his father's estate and his servants giving him healthy food.
- He was now putting on rags and was unkempt. He remembered his beautiful garments and the big closet he can make his choice of items of clothing.
- He was now begging the citizens of the land of his wild party to hire him. He remembered having many servants who are living as citizens of the land.
- He was now struggling for food with swine (not even with humans). He remembered the many delicacies he could not finish eating and the many foods he had given away.
- He was now living in the lowest form of abject poverty and humiliation. He remembered his authority and dignity in the land of his dominion.
- He was now begging strangers for just any food and a demeaning job. He remembered that he once had a voice of authority in the place of his dominion and the number of workers he had hired.
- He was now alone and lonely. He remembered the number of people that gathered around him—to eat at his table, to walk with him, to do business with his father, and just to attend a party at his house.

- The wild party was now over. He remembered the unending daily party his father always has.

He remembered how he asked for his inheritance from his father. He remembered the lies his friends told him to ditch his family and come pitch his tent with them. He remembered how he went far away from home with his friends. He remembered how he wasted all he had inherited on the wild party.

He remembered how all his friends left him when he had nothing left and then the famine struck the land. He remembered where he was coming from. He remembered where he was now. He remembered the great picture of the great future he saw when he was in his father's house.

Our God perfectly understands our past, knows our present, and unfathomably foreknows our future. Due to the impact of the past upon our present, even our future, our loving God calls us to first forget those ugly pasts then remember those beautiful moments.

God wants us to remember those romantic moments we once had with him, just like a man shared with his wife during the honeymoon and early years of marriage. What were you doing then that you are no longer doing now? Remember what you did for love. Let's go a little deeper into this aspect of remembering and forgetting.

Some people do remember to forget, while some just forget to remember.

Let me explain. Some folks remember their beautiful moments with God to forget their ugly past as victims. Some folks, however, forget their ugly past as victims to remember their beautiful moments with God. These are the categories of people God wants you to fall into.

However, some folks only remember their ugly moments as victims and thus forget those beautiful moments before they fell victims. They suddenly developed an emotional memory loss. And so they always live as victims. Sadly, some live like that all their lives, and more sadly, some had died that way—as victims.

Some folks forget their beautiful moments with God, and all that they remember were the ugly pasts that had made them victims.

And they always question God and tend to accuse God of abandoning them even for not forgiving them. And many had lived as victims all their lives.

However, there are some who tend to really forget what God had done for them. They forget how the Lord brought them up from dunghill to place them on the peak. They forget God's mercy and forgiveness. They forget that all they are now were not by their own might but by God's grace.

And when they now fall victims, they could no longer remember their God and his forgiveness. And so they lived in unforgiveness all their lives—unforgiving and unforgiven.

Likewise, when you remember those ugly pasts of which you were either the offender or the offended, God wants you to remember to forget it.

Let's hear God's charge on remembrance, especially in not forgetting God.

> You must obey all the commandments I give you today. If you do, you will not only live, you will multiply and will go in and take over the land promised to your fathers by the Lord.
>
> Do you remember how the Lord led you through the wilderness for all those forty years, humbling you and testing you to find out how you would respond, and whether or not you would really obey him? Yes, he humbled you by letting you go hungry and then feeding you with manna, a food previously unknown to both you and your ancestors. He did it to help you realize that food isn't everything and that real life comes by obeying every command of God.
>
> For all these forty years your clothes haven't grown old, and your feet haven't been blistered or swollen.
>
> So you should realize that, as a man punishes his son, the Lord punishes you to help you.

Obey the laws of the Lord your God. Walk in his ways and fear him. For the Lord your God is bringing you into a good land of brooks, pools, gushing springs, valleys, and hills; it is a land of wheat and barley, of grapevine, fig trees, pomegranates, olives, and honey; it is a land where food is plentiful, and nothing is lacking; it is a land where iron is as common as stone, and copper is abundant in the hills. When you have eaten your fill; bless the Lord your God for the good land he has given you.

But that is the time to be careful! Beware that in your plenty you don't forget the Lord your God and begin to disobey him. For when you have become full and prosperous and have built fine homes to live in, and when your flocks and herds have become very large, and your silver and gold have multiplied, that is the time to watch out that you don't become proud and forget the Lord your God who brought you out of your slavery in the land of Egypt. Beware that you don't forget the God who led you through the great and terrible wilderness with the dangerous snakes and scorpions, where it was so hot and dry. He gave you water from the rock! He fed you with manna in the wilderness (it was a kind of bread unknown before) so that you would become humble and so that your trust in him would grow, and he could do you good. He did it so that you would never feel that it was your own power and might that made you wealthy.

Always remember that it is the Lord your God who gives you the power to become rich, and he does it to fulfill his promise to your ancestors.

But if you forget about the Lord your God and worship other gods instead, and follow evil ways, you shall certainly perish, just as the Lord caused other nations in the past to perish. That will be your fate, too, if you don't obey the Lord your God. (Deuteronomy 8 TLB)

God wants you to remember. He is interested in those moments you once shared together. He remembers them and wants you to remember them too.

Again, the Lord spoke to me and said:
Go and shout this in Jerusalem's streets: The Lord says, "I remember how eager you were to please me as a young bride long ago, how you loved me and followed me even through the barren deserts. In those days Israel was a holy people, the first of my children. All who harmed them were counted deeply guilty and great evil fell on anyone who touched them." (Jeremiah 2:1–3 TLB)

Each one of us had a time or the other when we began our relationship with the Father, when our love for him was burning hot. Do you remember? Do you constantly remember how you came to know Christ and the first love you had for him? How is the initial love now? The young man remembered those days, times, and moments he had with his father.

Jesus had warned that, in the last days, the love of many shall wax cold, and many will fall out of grace and forget about their first love for God. It is for us to rise and not be a victim of this occurrence.

And many of you shall fall back into sin and betray and hate each other. And many false prophets will appear and lead many astray. Sin will be rampant everywhere and appear and cool

the love many. But those enduring to the end
shall be saved. (Matthew 24:10–13 TLB)

In order not to fall and remain victim, God calls you to remember. He wants you to remember your love for him and his love for you. He wants you to remember his mercy and goodness. He wants you to remember his tender mercies and loving-kindness. He wants you to remember his faithfulness.

God himself remembers all those moments we shared together with him. And he wants to bring back those moments, even make better moments.

Remember Where You Have Fallen

However, there is yet another aspect of *remember* that we need to talk about.

The Lord charged us in that book of Revelation to *remember therefore where you have fallen…*

There are some offenses that you might have forgotten, yet those you offended are still holding it against you deep down in their hearts. It may not be that they do not want to forgive you and let go, but you did not show remorse for your actions, or you just looked away. And they were hurting inside. And whenever they remember, they were filled with bitterness against you, and the heavens are not smiling at you either.

These folks, however, might be someone that has authority over you or spiritual ties with you. It may be your parents, children, siblings, spouse, friend, fellow Christian, or even pastor. The young man remembered all the people he had broken their hearts—his father, brother, servants, other friends, and people that have had connections with him one way or the other when he was still with his father.

The sad part is that you are not the only one who is hurting from this. The person holding that against you is also hurting from it. The Lord also charges you, the offended, to *remember therefore where you have fallen…*

You fail to let go because it hurts so deep. Fine. But do you know that you are causing so much pain and havoc to yourself than the offender? You may think because you fail to forgive him, he will have to suffer for the rest of his life. You think by holding it against her, she will not find peace forever.

Some had, however, quoted Jesus when he said, "Whosoever you forgive on earth is forgiven in heaven. And whosoever you withhold forgiveness on earth is withheld in heaven." (my own version).

> Whose soever sins ye remit, they are remitted unto them; and whose soever sins ye retain, they are retained. (John 20:23)

> If you forgive the sins of any, they are forgiven them; if you retain the sins of any, they are retained. (HCSB)

> If you forgive the sins of any, they are forgiven them; if you retain the sins of any, they are retained. (NKJV)

> If you forgive anyone's sins, they are forgiven. If you refuse to forgive them, they are unforgiven. (TLB)

Many of our spiritual leaders had taken it upon themselves to play the God in someone else's life by living out this passage of the Scripture under the false pretense that they had been offended.

This is common among some of our spiritual leaders. And they use this to bring fear into the lives of their followers so that nobody would offend them or question their (unbiblical and ungodly) actions even when they knew they were wrong. This is not the fear of God but the fear of the men of God. *These days, many are not parading themselves as the men of God but the gods of men. You have also fallen when you continue to hold offenses against a fellow human and vowed never to forgive him or her.*

Jesus had, however, emphasized that "But if ye do not forgive, neither will your Father which is in heaven forgive your trespasses" (Mark 11:26).

That is why God is calling you to remembrance and is now charging you to *remember therefore where you have fallen…*

Remember where you have played the God in the lives of your followers when you withheld forgiveness and placed them under a curse. Though it seems the heavens backed you up, the heaven of heavens still holds it against you that you had failed to forgive your fellow living being, especially when you had the chance to do so.

Get to read my other book, a series of six books, titled *Is Your Name Written There?* By God's grace, I laid much emphasis on this and some other critical spiritual leadership issues.

To both the offender and the offended, God is charging you today to *remember therefore where you have fallen…*

However, Jesus cannot force it on you. He can only call you to remember. He wants you to rise to a new beginning. The first principle needs to be applied. The first step needs to be taken. You must remember.

I wrote a beautiful poem titled "Don't Forget to Remember Me," and I am compiling some of my poems in a book of poetry, which I titled *Speechless.*

The question is, "Do I remember?" "What do I remember?"

> *I remember when my burdens rolled away,*
> *I had carried them for years, night and day,*
> *When I sought the blessed Lord,*
> *And I took Him at His word,*
> *Then at once all my burdens rolled away.*
>
> *Rolled away, rolled away*
> *I am happy since my burdens rolled away;*
> *Rolled away, rolled away,*
> *I am happy since my burdens rolled away.*

LET THE PARTY BEGIN!

I remember when my burdens rolled away,
That I feared would never leave night or day;
Jesus showed to me the loss,
So I left them at the cross;
I was glad when my burdens rolled away.

I remember when my burdens rolled away,
That had hindered me for years, night and day;
As I sought the throne of grace,
Just a glimpse of Jesus face,
And I knew that my burdens could not stay.

I am singing since my burdens rolled away,
There's a song within my heart night and day,
I am living for my king,
And with Joy I shout and sing.
Hallelujah! All my burdens rolled away.

—M. A. Steele

CHAPTER 8

PRINCIPLE TWO: REPENT

He *repented* of his bad past.

> I will go home to my father and say, "Father,
> I have sinned against both heaven and you, and
> am no longer worthy of being called your son.
> Please take me as a hired man." (Luke 15:18–19
> TLB)

Remembering the past alone does not really bring about the meaningful reclamation of lost dominion; even being sorrowful for it is not the end. Comparing the past with the present situation as to your devotion to God may have revealed some shameful backsliding. Sitting down to lick your wounds is not the solution. Covering it up is even more dangerous. You should take it to the Great Physician.

Personal medication cannot bring the desired healing. Let the Great Physician diagnose you and then prescribe your medication. That means you should return to God. And the next principle to apply as you rise to recover your lost dominion is *repentance*. Jesus charged us to *return and repent*.

> Think about those times of your first love
> (how different now!) and turn back to me again

and work as you did before; or else I will come and remove your candlestick from its place among the churches. (Revelations 2:5 TLB)

Jesus is calling you again, "Come back home." Jesus said in the parable that the father saw him from afar. It means the father had been waiting for his return. Every morning, he looks through the window. Every day, he sits at the porch. Every evening, he leaves the outside light on. Just as the father was waiting for the return of his son, the Lord is waiting for the return to dominion of those who have lost it and who have now gotten to their senses.

Softly and tenderly Jesus is calling,
Calling for you and for me,
See, on the portals, He's waiting and watching,
Watching for you and for me.

Come home, come home,
Ye who are weary, come home;
Earnestly, tenderly, Jesus is calling,
Calling, O sinner, come home!

Why should we tarry when Jesus is pleading
Pleading for you and for me?
Why should we linger and heed not His mercies
Mercies for you and for me?

Time is now fleeting, the moments are passing,
Passing for you and for me,
Shadows are gathering, death's night is coming,
Coming for you and for me?

O for the wonderful love He has promised,
Promised for you and for me!

Though we have sinned, He has mercy and pardon,
Pardon for you and for me.

—Will L. Thompson

You must stop running, stop hiding, and be honest with yourself. You cannot solve a problem with the same thinking and behaviors that created it; new thinking and actions are required. Change your mind. Change your directions. Change your actions.

Real dominion can only begin when you let God take control of the things that have taken control of you. You can only let God take control when you get to be open to him. You can only reclaim your lost dominion when you get to your senses and realize what you have lost. You cannot reclaim what you have not lost or what you claim to have not lost.

Your ugly past is not a determinant of your future. Your past cannot disqualify you from moving forward. It, however, can if you allow it. God always has more for you today than you lost yesterday. He has much more for you tomorrow than you are looking at today and will make you forget your yesterday.

You may, however, ask, "Can somebody with a bad past touch God in the present and his future be forever changed?" The answer is "yes."

You may say, "I've had several abortions because of my promiscuous life." "I've had a child out of wedlock." "I've cheated on my spouse." "I've become the black sheep of the family." "I've violated the trusts others placed in me." "I have been really bad and wicked." "I've been divorced." "I have sent innocent people to jail." "I've become the bad egg in the organization." "I've wrongly influenced gullible souls to their death and destruction." "I have caused so much pain to others." "I have broken many hearts." "I've been in prison." "I've caused the death of many." "I've ruined lives, families, marriages, and homes." "I've lost so much."

You may, however, say, "The ones I have offended are dead. Can I still find forgiveness?"

> I will go home to my father and say, "Father, I have sinned against both heaven and you, and I am no longer worthy of being called your son. Please take me on as a hired servant." (Luke 15:18–19 NLT)

The answer lies in this young man's experience. Many of those friends that went to the wild party with him were long dead, wasted, or living in destitution because of the famine. Many could not find their ways back home as he did. He broke the hearts of his father, brother, and servants, yet he did what Paul did. He puts all his effort to forget the past, seeking forgiveness with God and others and moving forward longing for what lies ahead of him.

He had even made up his mind that even if the father did not accept him as his son anymore, he would be okay just to become his servant. Though no good father would ever do that, this young man has made up his mind to return to the place of his dominion even if the position he once got had been occupied by another.

The bottom line is this, based on what the young man said about his return: In your return, your place might have been given to someone else. Return still because God will still welcome you and fix you up.

To Repent Is Not to Regret

Repentance should not be mistaken for regret. What some people feel is the regret that they had been caught and had to face the shame. Regret is not repentance. *Repentance is a turnaround, but regret is a look around.* God wants you to repent and not to regret. Repentance is what God honors and rewards because he is waiting for you to return to him.

The difference between Peter and Judas is what differentiates repent from regret. Peter repented and returned to Christ even after publicly denying him three times. He even cursed himself. Judas regretted and returned to his coconspirators and not to Jesus. Whom do you run back to determine the action you have taken—to repent or in regret.

There is, however, room for you at the cross. All that Christ needs from you is to rise above that past. And the next step to take after remembering is to repent and not live a life of regret.

Every sin has a past, and every sinner has a future. Let your past be your past and your future be your future.

Don't hide away from God. Be open to him. Let him see you and help you out. Let him see your wounds, and he will heal you. No matter how hard we try to hide the true conditions of our hearts from people, God knows how to make situations bring out our true colors and deal with our hypocritical attitudes if we do not repent on time.

God still invites the backsliding people. He is ready to forgive, restore, and bless you when you truly repent of your iniquities and return to him.

> If we say that we have no sin, we are only fooling ourselves and refusing to accept the truth. But if we confess our sins to him, he can be depended on to forgive us and to cleanse us from every wrong. (And it is perfectly proper for God to do this for us because Christ died to wash away our sins.) If we claim we have not sinned, we are lying and calling God a liar, for he says we have sinned. (1 John 1:8–10 TLB)

> *Jesus, I am coming home today,*
> *For I have found there's joy in thee alone,*
> *From the path of sin I turn away, Now*
> *I am coming home.*
>
> *Jesus, I am coming home today,*
> *Never, nevermore from Thee astray,*

Lord, I now accept Thy precious promise,
I am coming home.

Many years my heart has strayed from Thee,
And now repentant to Thy throne, I come;
Jesus opened up the way for me, Now
I am coming home.

Oh, the misery my sin has caused me,
Naught but pain and sorrow I have known,
Now I seek Thy saving grace and many,
I am coming home.

Fully trusting in Thy precious promise,
With no righteousness to call my own,
Pleading nothing but the blood of Jesus,
I am coming home.

Now I seek the cross where Jesus died!
For all my sins His blood will still atone,
Flowing o'er till ev'ry stain is covered,
I am coming home.

—A. H. Ackley

Please read David's testimony and challenge to us:

What happiness for those whose guilt has been forgiven! What joys when sins are covered over! What relief for those who have confessed their sins and God has cleared their record.

There was a time when I wouldn't admit what a sinner I was. But my dishonesty made me miserable and filled my days with frustration.

All day and all night your hand was heavy on me. My strength evaporated like water on a sunny day, until I finally admitted all my sins to you and stopped trying to hide them. I said to myself, "I will confess them to the Lord." And you forgave me! All my guilt is gone.

Now I say that each believer should confess his sins to God when he is aware of them, while there is time to be forgiven. Judgment will not teach him if he does. (Psalm 32:1–6 TLB)

Whether it's the guilt of something you have done or the pain of something that was done to you, it is time you let it go. Step into the river of God's mercy, and let it flow over you, setting you free from every unforgiving and unforgiven spirit.

Before you turn to God and stretch out your hands to him, get rid of your sins and leave all iniquity behind you. Only then, without the spots of sin to defile you, can you walk steadily forward to God without fear. Only then can you forget your misery. It will all be in the past. And your life will be cloudless; any darkness will be as bright as morning!

You will have courage because you will have hope. You will take your time and rest in safety. You will lie down unafraid, and many will look to you for help. (Job 11:13–19 TLB)

Is there any assurance as great as that? Free yourself off those shackles of guilt and shame. Repentance, however, is not just "feeling sorry" for what you have done wrong. It is a quality decision to break with the past and all its associations, pleasures, habits, and thought patterns. It is a turnaround. It is a turning point in your life.

Repentance is the positive change of your heart from ungodliness toward the Holy God. It is an absolute turnaround. It marks a turning point. True repentance affects intellect, emotion, and volition. Repentance is completely personal. You cannot repent for another person.

Repentance must not be misconceived for regret. What some people do is regret. They regret being caught in the act. They regret being exposed. They regret the mistakes of their being caught. That is why they go back with well-prepared acts to avoid being caught again and have covered up many sinful acts. They thought they were smart but never knew they were victims of self-imposed actions.

To Repent Is Not to Have Remorse

Repentance is different from being remorseful. You may feel remorseful, but it is not enough. You must add repentance to your remorse. Remorse would only say, "I'm sorry," but tend to repeat the same act. Remorse will want to correct the wrong but in the wrong direction. Regret looks around. Remorse looks back. Repentance looks inside, looks back, looks forward, and looks upward all at the same time because it is four-dimensional.

We need to understand the difference between a response and a reaction to an issue. If we would look deep inside, we will admit that most of the time, we tend to react to an issue as against responding to the same issue. When we respond, we face the issue to fight the issue. When we react, we face the person to attack him. Peter preached to thousands on the day of Pentecost, and the people responded with a question.

> Peter's words pierced their hearts, and they said to him and to the other apostles, "Brothers, what should we do?"
>
> Peter replied, "Each of you must repent of your sins and turn to God, and be baptized in the name of Jesus Christ for the forgiveness of your sins. Then you will receive the gift of the Holy Spirit. This promise is to you, to your children, and to those far away—all who have been called by the Lord our God." Then Peter contin-

ued preaching for a long time, strongly urging all his listeners, "Save yourselves from this crooked generation!"

Those who believed what Peter said were baptized and added to the church that day—about 3,000 in all. (Acts 2:37–41 NLT)

That was a response. That was repentance. The words of Peter not only gripped their souls but also touched their spirits. They repented, and the early church was birthed.

However, when Paul spoke the same word of truth to some others, they reacted, and a riot broke out.

The same thing happened in Iconium. Paul and Barnabas went to the Jewish synagogue and preached with such power that a great number of both Jews and Greeks became believers. Some of the Jews, however, spurned God's message and poisoned the minds of the Gentiles against Paul and Barnabas. But the apostles stayed there a long time, preaching boldly about the grace of the Lord. And the Lord proved their message was true by giving them power to do miraculous signs and wonders. But the people of the town were divided in their opinion about them. Some sided with the Jews, and some with the apostles.

Then a mob of Gentiles and Jews, along with their leaders, decided to attack and stone them. When the apostles learned of it, they fled to the region of Lycaonia—to the towns of Lystra and Derbe and the surrounding area. And there they preached the Good News. (Acts 14:1–7 NLT)

Remorse is an emotional reaction but always looks back. Repentance is a response to the message. It looks inside, backward, forward, and upward. God expects us to respond to the principle of repentance and not just to react to it.

The remorse of Judas Iscariot could not help him. He looked back at where he conspired to betray Jesus but never look inside at how he had allowed the devil to have a space in his heart and never looked upward to God in repentance.

> When Judas, who had betrayed him, realized that Jesus had been condemned to die, he was filled with remorse. So, he took the thirty pieces of silver back to the leading priests and the elders. "I have sinned," he declared, "for I have betrayed an innocent man."
>
> "What do we care?" they retorted. "That's your problem."
>
> Then Judas threw the silver coins down in the Temple and went out and hanged himself. The leading priests picked up the coins. "It wouldn't be right to put this money in the Temple treasury," they said, "since it was payment for murder." After some discussion, they finally decided to buy the potter's field, and they made it into a cemetery for foreigners. That is why the field is still called the Field of Blood. This fulfilled the prophecy of Jeremiah that says, "They took the thirty pieces of silver—the price at which he was valued by the people of Israel, and purchased the potter's field, as the LORD directed." (Matthew 27:3–10 NLT)

Judas felt remorse, left his accomplices with regret, and died as a victim—victim of evil prophesy, victim of selfishness and greed, victim of evil and selfish desires, victim of an evil conspiracy, victim of deceit, victim of betrayal, victim of circumstances.

> During this time, when about 120 believers were together in one place, Peter stood up and addressed them. "Brothers," he said, "the Scriptures had to be fulfilled concerning Judas, who guided those who arrested Jesus. This was predicted long ago by the Holy Spirit, speaking through King David. Judas was one of us and shared in the ministry with us." (Judas had bought a field with the money he received for his treachery. Falling headfirst there, his body split open, spilling out all his intestines. The news of his death spread to all the people of Jerusalem, and they gave the place the Aramaic name Akeldama, which means "Field of Blood.")
>
> Peter continued, "This was written in the book of Psalms, where it says, 'Let his home become desolate, with no one living in it.' It also says, 'Let someone else take his position'" (Acts 1:15–20 NLT)

It is only genuine repentance that will make you rise above your ugly past and make you a victor and not a victim.

The genuinely repentant attitude of Peter saved him from destruction. He repented, and the Lord received and restored him.

To Repent Is Not to Revenge

Repentance cannot be linked to vengeance. To repent does not mean to revenge. Samson had messed up the grace of God in his life. He lost his domination and fell into an abomination. The Philistines took advantage of his failure, captured him, took out his eyes that is the symbol of his vision, and chained him in prison for their entertainment.

Samson, however, regained his strength in the prison. God was expecting Samson to repent and then reclaim his dominion. Instead, Samson asked for revenge.

> So, the Philistines captured him and gouged out his eyes. They took him to Gaza, where he was bound with bronze chains and forced to grind grain in the prison. But before long, his hair began to grow back...
> Then Samson prayed to the LORD, "Sovereign LORD, remember me again. O God, please strengthen me just one more time. With one blow let me pay back the Philistines for the loss of my two eyes." Then Samson put his hands on the two center pillars that held up the temple. Pushing against them with both hands, he prayed, "Let me die with the Philistines." And the temple crashed down on the Philistine rulers and all the people. So, he killed more people when he died than he had during his entire lifetime. (Judges 16:21–22, 28–30 NLT)

You might have been made a victim out of your negligence and mistakes. You might have been made a victim and bear the consequence of your actions. God still expects you to repent and not to revenge. He that repents and returns to the Lord is automatically translated from the realm of painful judgment to the bliss of God's mercy. No matter what you have done, Jesus will not cast you out.

> Whoever comes to me, I will not cast out.
> (John 6:37)

But some will come to me—those the
Father has given me—and I will never, never
reject them. (John 6:37 TLB)

Tho' your sins are manifold
Jesus will not cast you out!
He's a friend, of love untold
Jesus will not cast you out!
God, to save us ev'ry one
Freely gave His only Son;
Come, whate'er you may have done
Jesus will not cast you out!

Tho' your spurn'd Him day by day
Jesus will not cast you out!
Come to Him—the Light, the Way
Jesus will not cast you out!
He will cleanse and make you whole;
Waves of sin may o'er you roll
He will save your deathless soul—
Jesus will not cast you out!

Grace is freely offer'd now—
Jesus will not cast you out!
At the cross, O wand'rer, bow
Jesus will not cast you out!
Come, nor turn again to sin!
Come, He bids you enter in!
Come and life eternal win!
Jesus will not cast you out!

—Geo Cooper

The Lord is close to those whose hearts are
breaking; he rescues those who are humbly sorry
for their sins. (Psalm 34:18 TLB)

Repentance involves you presenting yourself to God to thoroughly clean (on the outside) and cleanse (on the inside—a form of purging) you from every past. It involves presenting yourself for God to break you down, melt you, and remold you in his own way. Then he will fill you again to be useful for him.

I will love you to read Psalm 51 to better understand what I am saying. The breaking and remolding may be painful, but it is for your own good and to make you rise again.

> I will be patient while the Lord punishes me, for I have sinned against him, then he will defend me from my enemies and punish them for all the evil they have done to me. God will bring me out of my darkness into the light, and I will see his goodness. (Micah 7:9–11 TLB)

I challenge you today to kneel and pray to God. Tell him your sins, your pasts. Tell him your shame, your pains, your grief, your hurts. Show him the wounds, and ask him to come and heal you. Let him forgive you and make you whole again.

Hear him again. "Whoever comes to me, I will not cast out" (John 6:37).

Don't hold back. Tell him all. And you will rise into a new and healthy life. Amen.

CHAPTER 9

PRINCIPLE THREE: RECEIVE GOD'S GRACE AND GLORY

He *received* sufficient grace of God, and the glory of God overshadowed him. His father had been waiting for him.

> So, he returned home to his father. And
> while he was still a long distance away, his father
> saw him coming, and was filled with loving pity
> and ran and embraced and kissed him. (Luke
> 15:20 TLB)

God said, "My Grace is sufficient for you." He forgives as many times as you repent from your sin—because of the cross.

His grace will always forgive you. His grace will always be there for you to forget the past and look forward to what lies ahead. His grace will always be there to heal your wounds. His grace will always be there to turn your scars into stars. His grace will always be there to welcome you back to himself. His grace will always be sufficient for you. All you need to do is to receive the grace.

On his way back to the domain he belonged, he walked alone through the streets or roads he had once ridden on horses and with servants. The people may notice him, and some might have mocked

70

him, but he did not stop at them. He moved on to where he belonged. Some people could not recognize him because he has lost it all. He had nothing of repute on him again. Let us see what he might have lost:

- His garment
- His dignity
- His face
- His voice
- His inheritance
- His authority
- His name
- His status

On his way home, nobody could easily recognize him, but his father who had been waiting for him saw him from afar and ran toward him to welcome him back to the place of his dominion. That is what the grace of God does—to welcome you back to your dominion.

The grace of God carries his gifts and his goodness. He gives that without withdrawal even when such a person has left God or God has left him. That was what happened to King Saul. The grace of God to still reign as king over God's people was still on him even though the glory of God had left him long before.

That was what happened to Samson. The grace of God to still manifest and fight the enemies under the guise of the "anointing" was still on him, but the glory of God has left him.

That was what happened to Eli the priest and his sons. The grace of God to minister in the Temple and be the custodian and carrier of the Ark of the Covenant was still there, but the glory of God had left them. His daughter-in-law understood it when she gave birth to a son and named him Ichabod, which means the glory has departed (1 Samuel 4:22). The glory did not depart the day they died; the Glory had departed the day they left God to do what they knew was right (Read 1 Samuel 2–4)

This is a mystery that we need to understand. It is important to pray for the grace of God. It is much more essential to pray for the glory of God.

The grace of God carries his blessings. The glory of God carries his presence. The grace of God releases blessings from his hands. The glory of God causes his face to shine upon you. The grace of God carries the gifts of God based on the anointing of God.

The glory of God refreshes and releases the anointing every moment because of the presence of God. The grace of God can be seen and felt by people around you, and they even enjoy it with you. The glory of God is the way God sees you. The grace of God makes you get the title and the position. The glory of God makes you realize the title and position are not by your making but direct and sustain you in where God has placed you or allowed you to be placed.

The grace of God carries the presents from God. The glory of God carries the presence of God. The grace of God is God's freewill offering with no string attached. The glory of God is God offering himself with conditions attached. The glory of God carries the grace of God. But the grace of God does not always carry the glory of God. This is the mystery.

The grace of God has a limit to which it can be stretched, but the glory of God has no limit and cannot be quantified. Here is another issue: The grace of God carries the goodness of God, but the goodness of God sometimes never carries the grace of God.

That is the same goodness unbelievers and sinners enjoy. They seem to be blessed even when they commit sinful acts and get away with them. But the end justifies it all. However, we should not mistake the grace and goodness of God for the blessings of the devil. The devil also blesses and makes way for people to be blessed, and many had taken it as grace of God.

No, it is not the grace of God. It is God shutting his hands and his eyes and giving the people up for the devil to bless and to destroy. That is a great danger when God gives a person up and withholds his glory, grace, and goodness.

Are you only enjoying the goodness of God but are far from his grace? Are you enjoying the grace of God only but not experiencing the glory of God?

It is sad to say but so true that one may be anointed and still have been rejected by God. Yet some will still manifest the gifts and be used to perform miracles, sing, preach, and minister to lives.

The goodness of God can be wasted, the grace of God can be lost, and the glory of God can be taken away.

> O Lord, please help my life that your glory and grace will not depart from me.
>
> O Lord, I pray that your grace will always be my portion. I also pray more especially that your glory will always rest upon me and not depart from my life. Help me, Lord, not to waste your glory. Help me, O Lord, that your glory is not taken away from me. Whatever I will do to that will make me lose your glory and grace. O Lord, help me not to lay hands and heart on them. Whatever would make me waste your grace or allow your glory to be taken away from me, O Lord, destroy them in me and around me. Your glory carries your grace. Let your glory and grace rest upon me, O Lord. In Jesus's name, I pray. Amen.

The glory of God is embedded in the grace of God. But the grace of God does not always carry the glory of God. The grace of God is when God opens his hands to you. The glory of God is when God opens his eyes and shines his face upon you. The glory of God is the reflection of God's presence that illuminates and radiates even the grace of God.

The grace of God is the reflection of God's blessings whether you deserve it or not and does not always or necessarily carry the glory of God. The grace of God can rest on anyone. The glory of

God only rests on the dependable and acceptable, not just the able, capable, or available.

Are you dependable and acceptable to carry the glory of God? Can God trust you with his glory, or has he just left you with only his grace? Or has God left you without grace and glory but just enjoying only the goodness?

You cannot carry the glory of God and not carry the grace of God. You cannot carry the grace of God without carrying the goodness of God. But you can carry the grace of God and still not carry the glory of God.

The grace of God will make the world recognize you. The glory of God will make God recognize you.

I'd rather long for the glory of God than only bask in the grace of God without his glory. I'd rather let God shine his face upon me and see his glory in my life than men to only applaud the grace of God upon me. I'd rather cry as Moses cried to God in Exodus 33; if your presence does not go with me, do not let me leave for anywhere than just carry grace and enjoy only the grace.

> So, he returned home to his father. And while he was still a long distance away, his father saw him coming, and was filled with loving pity and ran and embraced and kissed him. (Luke 15:20 TLB)

I want you to take note of some important issues here. When this young man left home, he was not alone. He went with some friends. However, when he was returning home, he returned alone. Two things I want to bring out from this:

- Satan's destruction is collective, but Christ's redemption is individual (John 3:16). However, we must not misunderstand revival for redemption. Revival is collective. However, revival should lead to individual redemption. Revival is not salvation. A church can be revived yet still have some unsaved members. Do not just enjoy the revival, but be part of the redemption.

Salvation is a personal decision that you must make to receive the grace of God. Nobody would decide your salvation for you, but many can decide your destruction and damnation for you if you allow them. The devil is good at organizing collective destructions. Who knows what could have happened to other young folks like him when the wild party was over and there was no money left. "The thief's purpose is to steal and kill and destroy. My purpose is to give life in all its fullness" (John 10:10 NLT)

- He could have been a source of influence on other young folks as many had become the voice of destruction to other young folks all in the name of being role models and social media influencers. He led many young folks away from their dominion to their destruction. However, he returned alone.

  He could not come along with others that went with him. That is why you should not let the one that does not know where he is going decide your direction. You should not let the one heading to nowhere in life determine your destination. He got his own turning point, but it has become too late for others that went with him.

The grace worked for him because he got back to his senses, and he applied the principles for new beginning. Many could not get to this point. They had died along the way.

> O Lord, my God and my Maker, even when
> I could not see your hands, always shine your face
> upon me. Do not close your eyes of glory on me
> even when you open your hands of grace to me.
> Help me not just to only showcase your grace
> without feeling the presence of your glory. Because
> when I can still see your face, then I can always see
> your hands. In Jesus's name, I pray. Amen.

They that trust in the Lord are secure,
Tho' the storm rages dark o'er the sea,
For this anchor of promise is sure
"My Grace is sufficient for thee."

"My grace is sufficient for thee,"
"My grace is sufficient for thee,"
Oh, matchless, boundless grace of God,
"My grace is sufficient for thee!"

What a boon to the pilgrim oppress,
What a balm such a promise must be
To the laden ones seeking for rest,
"My grace is sufficient for thee."

In the race for the prize, fainting soul,
Though a weary you bow down the knee,
Rise again, and press on the goal,
"My grace is sufficient for thee."

Neither trial nor doubt brings dismay,
Nor from danger that comes will I feel;
For I stand on this promise today
"My grace is sufficient for thee."

—C. M. Robinson

O Lord, I immerse myself into that grace today. Let your grace be sufficient for me. Let your grace heal me of my past, make me forget my past, and give me a glorious future to look forward to. In Jesus's name, I pray. Amen!

Principle Four: Make Restitution

He made *restitution*.

> His son said to him, "Father, I have sinned against heaven and you, and am not worthy of being called your son." (Luke 15:21 TLB)

This is where you take responsibility for your reclamation. This is where you break that barrier your past has placed on you. The true basis of all inner healing rests in our willingness to forgive and, when possible, to make amends to those we have hurt. That is also true for reclaiming your lost dominion.

Zacchaeus was a perfect example of this issue. Though he was a Jew, Zacchaeus worked for the system that enslaved his own people. He collected taxes for the Romans. Tax collectors were among the most hated people in Palestine then because they usually extort more than the system demanded and enriched themselves doing it.

However, when Jesus said to Zacchaeus, "Quick! Come down! For I am going to be a guest in your home today" (Luke 19:5 TLB), everybody was shocked.

It is a wonderful thing to be adopted and acknowledged by God. He accepts the unaccepted. He forgives the unforgivable and the unforgiven. He welcomes the unwelcome. He looks for the unwanted. He gives victory to the victimized. He gives mercy to the culprit.

He gives his name to the nameless. He gives his face to the faceless. He gives his voice to the voiceless. He makes their scoffers go speechless. He gives his heart to the heartless. He paid the price for the worthless. He removes the shame of the past. He turns scars into stars.

No wonder sinners loved him. No wonder he stopped because of many who never deserved it. His name is praised forever.

The Bible makes no mention of what Jesus said to Zacchaeus over the supper that night. But I am sure those words brought healing to his soul. Those words brought forgiveness into his life. Those words turned him from culprit into a conqueror.

Those words turned him from a victim into a victor. Those words turned him from the unforgiving and unforgiven to be forgiven. Those words turned him from the man with abomination to the man with domination. Those words were so soothing that the man, once upon a time a conman, cried out, "Sir, from now on I will give half my wealth to the poor, and if I have overcharged anyone on his taxes, I will penalize myself by giving him back four times as much" (Luke 19:8 TLB).

Jesus heard his confessions, saw the sincerity of his heart, and added, "This shows that salvation has come to this home today. This man was one of the lost sons of Abraham, and I, the Messiah have come to search for and to save such souls as his" (Luke 19:9–10 TLB).

Let us look at some steps we, like Zacchaeus, can take for restitution:

- Talk to God before talking to the person.
- Always take the first step.
- Sympathize with other people's feelings.
- Attack the problem, not the person.
- Fulfill your own part as much as possible.

- Focus on reconciliation and not resolution.

Talk to God before Talking to the Person

Talk with God first. Discuss the problem with God first before talking to any other person. When the young man came to his senses, he literally talked to God before he rose to return to his father. When he got to his father, he repeated what he had rehearsed with God to his father.

> When he finally came to his senses, he said to himself, "At home, even the hired servants have food enough to spare, and here I am dying of hunger! I will go home to my father and say, 'Father, I have sinned against both heaven and you, and I am no longer worthy of being called your son. Please take me on as a hired servant.'"
>
> So, he returned home to his father. And while he was still a long way off, his father saw him coming. Filled with love and compassion, he ran to his son, embraced him, and kissed him. His son said to him, "Father, I have sinned against both heaven and you, and I am no longer worthy of being called your son." (Luke 15:17–20 NLT)

That was what Zacchaeus also did. He had a talk with Jesus before taking the steps for his restitution. If at first you pray about the conflict instead of complaining to a friend or other party, you will often discover that either God changes your heart or he changes the heart of the other person without your help. And most times, he does both.

All broken and strained relationships would be restored if you would just pray more about them than only nag and complain.

Tell God your fault if you are the offender and your frustration if you are the one offended. Cry out to him. Tell God how you really feel. No one else can help you out except God. It is God that will direct your steps on what to do and speak. It was after the young man talked to God that he was able to talk to his father. It was after Zacchaeus's meeting with Jesus that he voiced out his steps of restitution.

Always Take the First Step

Always take the initiative, whether you are the offender or the offended. God expects you to make the first move no matter which side of the offense you find yourself. Don't wait for the other party. Go to them first.

This applied to both the young man and his father. The young man took the step to return. The father saw him from afar and did not wait for him to get home and start asking questions on where he has been and why was he coming back and what is he coming to do as some would do. The father ran to meet him when he saw him from afar.

> So, he returned home to his father. And while he was still a long way off, his father saw him coming. Filled with love and compassion, he ran to his son, embraced him, and kissed him.

This principle and steps of restitution are so important that Jesus emphasized that it takes priority over corporate and individual worship.

Jesus said, "So if you are standing before the altar in the Temple, offering a sacrifice to God, and suddenly remember that a friend has something against you, leave your sacrifice there beside the altar and go and apologize and be reconciled to him, and then come and offer your sacrifice to God" (Matthew 5:23–24 TLB).

Do not procrastinate in your steps for restitution. Delay may be dangerous. Delays only widen the wounds, deepen resentments, and make matters worse. When you act on time, it also reduces the spiritual damage on you. Aside from making us emotionally miserable, the Bible says unresolved conflicts block our fellowship with God and keep our prayers from being answered.

> You husbands must be careful of your wives, being thoughtful of their needs and honoring them as the weaker sex. Remember that you and your wife are partners in receiving God's blessings, and if you don't treat her as you should, your prayers will not get ready answers. (1 Peter 3:7 TLB)

> God doesn't listen to the prayers of those who flout the laws. (Proverbs 28:9 TLB)

And in taking this step, choose the right time and place. Zacchaeus did it when Jesus came to his house, and all witnessed it, including his haters. This young prodigal openly asked for his inheritance and ditched everyone to their faces. He came back openly too, not at night to hide from people. The father saw him left in public and ran to welcome him back in public too.

You do not offend people in public and expect to apologize in private to cover up your shame. You did it in the open, so let it be undone in the open too.

Let the people, at least if not all of them, who saw what you did as an offense also see what you did as restitution. It goes a long way to bring hope into the heart of the offended and build the trust of both the offended and the witnesses in you. The servants witnessed the open reconciliation between the father and son and were able to relay the message to the older brother.

> Meanwhile, the older son was in the fields working. When he returned home, he heard music and dancing in the house, and he asked one of the servants what was going on. "Your brother is back," he was told, "and your father has killed

the fattened calf. We are celebrating because of
his safe return." (Luke 15:25–27 NLT)

It does not make you a fool; instead, it makes you wiser and
builds you stronger. You are not stupid for doing that. You are saving
lives and yours inclusive.

Sympathize with Other People's Feelings

Be a good listener rather than a complainer. Before attempting
to make a resolution or accept restitution, you must first listen to
people's feelings. Focus on their feelings and not on your judgment.
Do not try to talk people out of their feelings at first. Just listen to
them, and let them unload emotionally without being defensive.

Confess your own part of the conflict. If you are serious about
making the steps for restitution, you should begin by admitting your
own mistakes.

His son said to him, "Father, I have sinned
against both heaven and you, and I am no longer
worthy of being called your son." (Luke 15:21
NLT)

We, most times, are blinded to some faults on our part in cases
of offense and broken relationships. Ask God to show you how much
of the problem is your fault. Also, you need to ask a third party to
help you evaluate your own actions before meeting with the person
with whom you have a conflict.

We may be seeing a speck in the eyes of others through the
unnoticed log we have in our eyes. But Jesus told us to first remove
the log from our own before taking out the speck from another person's eye (Matthew 7:5).

A confession is a powerful tool for reconciliation and restitution. If we must admit, we would accept that often, the way we han-
dle a conflict creates a bigger hurt than the original problem itself.
When you, however, begin by humbly admitting your mistakes, it

defuses the other person's anger and disarms their attacks because they were probably expecting you to be defensive.

Honestly own up to any part you have played in the conflict, and do not make excuses or shift blame. It is for you to accept responsibility for your mistakes and ask for forgiveness. The prodigal son took this step and returned to his father. Paul took this step as he went back to the folks he had persecuted.

Zacchaeus also took this step as he voiced to pay back four times all he had extorted from his people. And we did not read of any further resentment against Zacchaeus after that encounter.

Attack the Problem, Not the Person

You cannot fix the problem if you are consumed with fighting the people. You cannot fix the problem if you are consumed with shifting the blame. You cannot fix the offense if you are consumed with flexing muscles with the offender. You must choose between the two.

Look beyond the person behind the issue. Look at the issue behind the person.

> His son said to him, "Father, I have sinned against both heaven and you, and I am no longer worthy of being called your son."
> But his father said to the servants, "Quick! Bring the finest robe in the house and put it on him. Get a ring for his finger and sandals for his feet. And kill the calf we have been fattening. We must celebrate with a feast, for this son of mine was dead and has now returned to life. He was lost, but now he is found." So, the party began.
> (Luke 15:21–24 NLT)

It was not that the father overlooked what his son had done. It was not that the father covered it up either. His father did not attack him for wasting all he had inherited. His father saw him as once blind but now could see. His father saw him as once lost but now was found. His father saw him as once away but now back home.

His father saw him as once dead but now back to life. When you look beyond the person, you will see the problem. Most of the time, parents have faults in this. Spouses are also guilty of this. Many employers are guilty of this. Even some pastors are guilty of this.

We have lost the best of people in our lives and have destroyed the best of relationships God has blessed us with when we attack the person and had no understanding of the issue behind the person.

Let God open your eye to the real issue behind the person, and that is what you should face and help fix. That was the example Jesus gave concerning Zacchaeus's issue when he declared, "This man was one of the lost sons of Abraham, and I, the Messiah have come to search for and to save such souls as his" (Luke 19:10 TLB).

Jesus did not lash out at Zacchaeus for cheating on his fellow Jews but spoke kindly to him even after Zacchaeus had taken his steps for restitution. Jesus called the same man that the Jews called an outcast one of the lost sons of Abraham.

Apostle Paul sums it up this way:

> If anyone is stealing, he must stop it and begin using those hands of his for honest work so he can give to others in need. Don't use bad language. Say only what is good and helpful to those you are talking to, and what will give them a blessing. (Ephesians 4:28–29 TLB)

You are never persuasive when you are abrasive and abusive. Look beyond the person. Look at the problem.

Fulfill Your Own Part as Much as Possible

Peace has a price tag. Restitution demands sacrifice. God expects you to fulfill your own part of the reconciliation by cooperating with the directives of the Holy Spirit. The young man came to his father and begged for forgiveness. The father settled it with him right there, and the party began right there. The father did not postpone it for another time when he would be in good mood to welcome his son home. He did it right away.

> His son said to him, "Father, I have sinned against both heaven and you, and I am no longer worthy of being called your son."
> But his father said to the servants, "Quick! Bring the finest robe in the house and put it on him. Get a ring for his finger and sandals for his feet. And kill the calf we have been fattening. We must celebrate with a feast, for this son of mine was dead and has now returned to life. He was lost, but now he is found." So, the party began.
> (Luke 15:21–24 NLT)

The Bible charged us to "Be at peace with everyone just as much as possible" (Romans 12:18 TLB).

Sometimes, it costs our pride; most times, it costs our self-centeredness. Let go and let God. The father said that his son that was lost has been found. His son that was dead has been restored to life.

Zacchaeus was no longer remembered as the cheat but as the man who had Jesus as his houseguest. They no longer called him an outcast but one of the lost sons of Abraham that has been found. What an encounter it was. And the rest, as they say, was history.

Focus on Reconciliation and Not Resolution

The principle of restitution is to focus on reconciliation and not resolution. You reconcile a relationship, not resolve a problem. Your focus should not be to resolve a problem though you had been advised to look at the problem behind the person as you tackle the issue. Your focus should largely be to reconcile and restore a relationship.

> His son said to him, "Father, I have sinned against both heaven and you, and I am no longer worthy of being called your son."
>
> But his father said to the servants, "Quick! Bring the finest robe in the house and put it on him. Get a ring for his finger and sandals for his feet. And kill the calf we have been fattening. We must celebrate with a feast, for this son of mine was dead and has now returned to life. He was lost, but now he is found. So, the party began. (Luke 15:21–24 NLT)

The young man went back to restore their relationship. He did not go there to start telling stories, giving excuses, and looking for empathy. And the father too worked to restore the relationship. When you focus on the reconciliation, the resolution will be fixed. Jesus did not come to resolve the troubles of the world. He came to reconcile us with God.

> Come now, and let us reason together, saith the LORD: though your sins be as scarlet, they shall be as white as snow; though they be red like crimson, they shall be as wool. (Isaiah 1:18)

> "Come now, let us settle the matter," says the LORD. "Though your sins are like scarlet, they shall be as white as snow; though they are red as crimson, they shall be like wool." (NIV)

> Come now and let's deliberate over the next steps to take together. Yahweh promises you over and over: "Though your sins stain you like scarlet, I will whiten them like bright, new-fallen

snow! Even though they are deep red like crimson, they will be made white like wool!" (TPT)

Come, let's talk this over, says the Lord; no matter how deep the stain of your sins, I can take it out and make you as clean as freshly fallen snow. Even if you are stained as red as crimson, I can make you white as wool! (TLB)

"Come now, let's settle this," says the LORD. "Though your sins are like scarlet, I will make them as white as snow. Though they are red like crimson, I will make them as white as wool." (NLT)

That was what Jesus also did in the house of Zacchaeus. He did not go there to fix a problem but to restore a relationship. If Jesus was to fix a problem, he would have to fix the tax issues and oppressions with the Romans, fix discrimination issues with the Jewish leaders, fix the socioeconomic issues with the system, and fix religious issues with the Jews. Jesus, however, came to restore the lost souls to God.

This man was one of the lost sons of Abraham, and I, the Messiah have come to search for and to save such souls as his. (Luke 19:10 TLB)

Jesus did not call Zacchaeus a cheat or an enemy (because Zacchaeus was working for the Romans against the Jews), but Jesus said that he was one of the lost sons of Abraham who along with others needed salvation. *When we focus on reconciliation, the problem loses significance and often becomes irrelevant because it will surely be solved.*

Not All Reconciliation Means Reunion

However, there is a caveat to this issue. There are some reconciliations that would and should not be allowed to lead to a reunion. The fact that you have forgiven someone and had reconciled does not mean there should be a reunion. Some reconciliation should be done with a distance.

I will say there is reconciliation in separation. It does not mean you have not forgiven, but you just need to move on with your life and without them in your life again. This is harsh but the truth, the whole truth, and nothing but the truth.

You do not form a reunion with someone who had earlier wanted you dead just because you escaped by the grace of God. You do not form any reunion with the family member that raped you and violated your dignity. You do not form any reunion with someone that almost ran you over with his vehicle. You do not form a reunion with someone who had earlier poisoned your drink, your food, or your prestige before the world.

To better understand this let us delve into the Bible.

Joseph reconciled with his brothers, but he no longer formed any reunion with them. He let them be on their own, and he lived his own life on his own. They were still brothers, but that is all they would be to him. He would not call them up to share any dream with them again. That is not hatred. That is not resentment. That is applying wisdom.

> Joseph could stand it no longer. There were many people in the room, and he said to his attendants, "Out, all of you!" So, he was alone with his brothers when he told them who he was. Then he broke down and wept. He wept so loudly the Egyptians could hear him, and word of it quickly carried to Pharaoh's palace.
>
> "I am Joseph!" he said to his brothers. "Is my father still alive?" But his brothers were speechless! They were stunned to realize that Joseph was

standing there in front of them. "Please, come closer," he said to them. So, they came closer. And he said again, "I am Joseph, your brother, whom you sold into slavery in Egypt. But don't be upset, and don't be angry with yourselves for selling me to this place. It was God who sent me here ahead of you to preserve your lives. This famine that has ravaged the land for two years will last five more years, and there will be neither plowing nor harvesting. God has sent me ahead of you to keep you and your families alive and to preserve many survivors.

"So it was God who sent me here, not you! And he is the one who made me an adviser to Pharaoh—the manager of his entire palace and the governor of all Egypt.

"Now hurry back to my father and tell him, 'This is what your son Joseph says: God has made me master over all the land of Egypt. So come down to me immediately! You can live in the region of Goshen, where you can be near me with all your children and grandchildren, your flocks and herds, and everything you own. I will take care of you there, for there are still five years of famine ahead of us. Otherwise, you, your household, and all your animals will starve.'" (Genesis 45:1–11 NLT)

Joseph had reconciled with his brothers. They had lived in the same land that Joseph gave them. He did not tell them to come and live in the palace with him. However, after many years and Jacob, their father, had died, the brothers were still scared of him.

They realized that he only reconciled with them but did not reunite with them. So they came because they thought he still had resentment against them. But Joseph made them understand that it was for the good of everyone.

> After burying Jacob, Joseph returned to Egypt with his brothers and all who had accompanied him to his father's burial. But now that their father was dead, Joseph's brothers became fearful. "Now Joseph will show his anger and pay us back for all the wrong we did to him," they said.
>
> So they sent this message to Joseph: "Before your father died, he instructed us to say to you: 'Please forgive your brothers for the great wrong they did to you—for their sin in treating you so cruelly.' So we, the servants of the God of your father, beg you to forgive our sin." When Joseph received the message, he broke down and wept. Then his brothers came and threw themselves down before Joseph. "Look, we are your slaves!" they said.
>
> But Joseph replied, "Don't be afraid of me. Am I God, that I can punish you? You intended to harm me, but God intended it all for good. He brought me to this position so I could save the lives of many people. No, don't be afraid. I will continue to take care of you and your children." So he reassured them by speaking kindly to them.
>
> So Joseph and his brothers and their families continued to live in Egypt. Joseph lived to the age of 110. (Genesis 50:14–22 NLT)

Reconciliation is not resentment. But not all reconciliation should lead to a reunion. This is for the good of everyone involved. Your life should move on. Life will not be the same again. You can still be seeing them around you, but they are no longer with you.

You do not need to go back to those friends again. You do not need to go back to that house again. You do not need to go back to that relationship again. You do not need to go back to that church, yes that church again. Let God order your step and lead you aright. You have reconciled with them, but you do not need to go back to them.

Saul grew so envious of David that he wanted him dead. He even went as far as chasing after David to the wilderness. When David caught up with King Saul and spared his life, David forgave him but never formed any reunion. David went his own way and never returned to the palace with King Saul.

Saul recognized David's voice and called out, "Is that you, my son David?"

And David replied, "Yes, my lord the king. Why are you chasing me? What have I done? What is my crime? But now let my lord the king listen to his servant. If the LORD has stirred you up against me, then let him accept my offering. But if this is simply a human scheme, then may those involved be cursed by the LORD. For they have driven me from my home, so I can no longer live among the LORD's people, and they have said, 'Go, worship pagan gods.' Must I die on foreign soil, far from the presence of the LORD? Why has the king of Israel come out to search for a single flea? Why does he hunt me down like a partridge on the mountains?"

Then Saul confessed, "I have sinned. Come back home, my son, and I will no longer try to harm you, for you valued my life today. I have been a fool and very, very wrong."

"Here is your spear, O king," David replied. "Let one of your young men come over and get it. The LORD gives his own reward for doing good and for being loyal, and I refused to kill you even when the LORD placed you in my power, for you are the LORD's anointed one. Now may the LORD value my life, even as I have valued yours today. May he rescue me from all my troubles." And Saul said to David, "Blessings on you, my son David. You will do many heroic deeds, and you will surely succeed." Then David went away, and Saul returned home. (1 Samuel 26:17–25 NLT)

Some places are not worth your return. It is not resentment. The problem has been resolved. There is reconciliation. But it is not worth your reunion. Some people are not worth your return. Your return could be like what the Bible says that the dog has gone back to his vomit. Your return could cause more danger to you. This time, you may not live to tell the story.

As a dog returns to its vomit, so a fool repeats his foolishness. (Proverbs 26:11 NLT)

They prove the truth of this proverb: "A dog returns to its vomit." And another says, "A washed pig returns to the mud." (2 Peter 2:22 NLT)

God warned the young prophet not to go back to the palace. When he was later deceived by the old prophet to return to his house, he faced the consequence.

When King Jeroboam heard the man of God speaking against the altar at Bethel, he pointed at him and shouted, "Seize that man!" But instantly the king's hand became paralyzed in that position, and he couldn't pull it back. At the same time a wide crack appeared in the altar, and the ashes poured out, just as the man of God had predicted in his message from the LORD.

The king cried out to the man of God, "Please ask the LORD your God to restore my hand again!" So the man of God prayed to the LORD, and the king's hand was restored and he could move it again. Then the king said to the man of God, "Come to the palace with me and have something to eat, and I will give you a gift." But the man of God said to the king, "Even if you gave me half of everything you own, I would not go with you. I would not eat or drink anything in this place. For the LORD gave me this command: 'You must not eat or drink anything while you are there, and do not return to Judah by the same way you came.'" So he left Bethel and went home another way. (1 Kings 13:4–10 NLT)

God warned the wise men from the east not to return to the palace of Herod after telling him about the newborn king whose star they had traced to the palace. King Herod had told them to come back to tell him after they had found the baby.

Then Herod called for a private meeting with the wise men, and he learned from them the time when the star first appeared. Then he told them, "Go to Bethlehem and search carefully for the child. And when you find him, come back and tell me so that I can go and worship him, too!" After this interview, the wise men went their way. And the star they had seen in the east guided them to Bethlehem. It went ahead of them and stopped over the place where the child was. When they saw the star, they were filled with joy! They entered the house and saw the child with his mother, Mary, and they bowed down and worshiped him. Then they opened their treasure chests and gave him gifts of gold, frankincense, and myrrh. When it was time to leave, they returned to their own country by another route, for God had warned them in a dream not to return to Herod. (Matthew 2:7–12 NLT)

Nevertheless, let's come back to the issue of the prodigal son. This young man was the one at fault. He left his place of dominion. He got back to his senses, and he returned to where he belonged. There is a place waiting for your reconciliation too.

Zacchaeus also rose above his pasts and into a new beginning. He accepted God's forgiveness, accepted people's forgiveness, forgave others, and forgave himself. And he rose to a new beginning. He became a new man. For you to reclaim your lost dominion, your responsibility is needed.

You will need to confess to those you have hurt, offended, and wounded. You will need to even make restitution. Some may know that you did it. Some may not know that you did it. Some may never have the knowledge that you caused it. But it is you who carry that pain the most. In your confession, you are breaking the barrier that hinders your reclamation, and you are rising to a new beginning. Read again the words Jesus spoke to Zacchaeus:

This man was one of the lost sons of Abraham, and I, the Messiah have come to search for and to save such souls as his. (Luke 19:10)

Jesus on Calvary died in my place,
Saved to the uttermost, wonderful grace.
I saw him lifted up,
My heart He drew old things have passed away,
All things are new.

Old things have passed away, All things are new,
Old things have passed away, All things are new;
Jesus my Saviour, saves me thro' and thro'
Old things have passed away, All things are new.

LET THE PARTY BEGIN!

Tho' I was far away, He saw my need,
His spirit touched my heart, caused me to plead
His name above all names, His work so true.
Old things have passed away,
All things are new.

My heart in tune with His, Fellowship
His Joy He gives to me, my Joy complete.
Thro' all eternity, His face I'll view,
Old things have passed away,
All things are new.

—S. Cox

CHAPTER 11

PRINCIPLE FIVE: RENOUNCE YOUR PAST

He *renounced* his past.

> I will go home… Please forgive me… I have sinned against heaven and you… Please take me…" (Luke 15:18–19 NLT)

Those were his statement. He put in all his energies to forget the past and look forward to a better future. He concluded that even if he is not welcomed as a son, he still wanted to be welcomed back home perhaps as a servant. He turned his back and never looked back.

When a man fails, falters, or falls and refuses to rise above what made him fall, he opens himself to things like fear, shame, insecurity, resentment, and rejection. When you fail to deal with the issues, you give them chance to further and deeper take control of your life.

However, to rise to a new beginning and reclaim your lost dominion, you must follow the fifth principle—*renounce your past.*

It is not only healthy to express your emotions in the right way. It is in fact self-destructive not to.

Jesus said, "Blessed are they that mourn: for they shall be comforted" (Matthew 5:4). Jesus wants you to pour out your heart to him. He wants you to tell him your pain and show him the wounds.

However, when you try to bottle up emotions and hide your wounds, they just drop from your conscious into your subconscious, and what you had refused to deal with then begin to deal with you. It had been discovered and proven that many folks who had emotional traumas are easily afflicted with physical ailments and are quickly killed by such ailments.

The emotional pains that are not dealt with will always weaken the body system and give room for some physical pains. The sad part is that some of these physical pains may not be deadly, but the emotional pains had made it deadly for the victims.

It is obvious. Even in the natural body, if you continue to hide your physical wounds and are not open for treatment, you will always have pain. And that pain could lead to decay or deformity. It would affect all other parts of the body including your brain. You now see to what extent a little wound that is not treated could go.

That is to what extent an ugly part of your past could go if you fail to renounce it. It could ruin your life and terminate your future. Some folks have made the mistake of covering their pasts to forget it. They hide it inside of them but still remember it sometimes. But it becomes a trust issue when the people they tried to hide it from got to discover it later.

The old hymn says, "I was once lost but now I'm found; Was blind but now I see." You cannot renounce what you cannot review. You must review it to renounce it. You cannot renounce what you want to hide. What you fail to renounce will find a way to announce itself. And that may be destructive.

Do not hide your wounds. Be open to your healer. Let him bind it for you. When the wound is healed even if it leaves a scar, it no longer becomes a pain but something you have been able to overcome. You cannot self-medicate what the doctor has not prescribed.

Mike Murdock once said, "You cannot correct what you are unwilling to confront."

What you fail to confront will one day confront you. Those emotions you fail to deal with will eventually begin to deal with you. And then you will begin to look out for ways to overcome them—which they will also dictate for you.

That is the reason why many folks turn to drugs, alcoholism, smoking, being workaholic, overeating, promiscuity, sex, substance abuse, and other forms of compulsive or aberrant behaviors just to escape from those pains and wounds. Addiction is never the solution to the pain that is affecting your emotion. However, these forms of escapism only worsen the pain, widen the wounds, and compound the bitterness.

Little wonder, a victim of child abuse would end up becoming violent and joining gangs. Little wonder, a victim of rejection would end up a rapist or prostitute. Little wonder, a victim of disappointment would end up a drunkard or alcoholic.

Little wonder, a victim of rape would end up a drug addict or prostitute. Little wonder, a victim of sex abuse would end up being promiscuous and resentful. Little wonder, a victim of divorce would end up a workaholic and have no time for his or her children or for any relationship.

Little wonder, a victim of a broken relationship would end up in loneliness and depression. Little wonder, a victim of false accusation would end up in bitterness and become a sadist. Little wonder, a victim of depression would end up committing suicide.

Some of the things we need to rise from and rise above are so deeply rooted in us that they have moved from our conscious to our subconscious. We suffer their effects, yet we do not understand their cause. That is why we need God to bring them to the surface and help us deal with them one by one.

You cannot renounce what you do not want to review. You cannot correct what you do not want to confront. Whoever wants to announce the past you have renounced against you has a big problem, but that is their problem, not yours. You have renounced it and have moved forward. God has a way of using their announcement to announce your new beginning too.

Take a deeper look at yourself. You weren't a drunkard before. It started the day after you were rejected, were disappointed, lost your job, failed your marriage, or failed in business. It started the day you were advised to clear your mind off those pains and memories and "make yourself happy."

A form of escapism, right? Wrong! You weren't a gangster, prostitute, smoker, or drug addict before. It all started after you fell victim and you wanted something that could make you feel happy. And you had thought, *Just one dose, one cup, one time-out, one one-night stand.* Just one will do and take away those pain and shame and bring you back to your normal self. But it never does and never will do.

And you found out that one is never enough. The memories continued to linger, and so did your escapism. Then and there, you become addicted. Yet the pains and shame of that ugly past remain. And both the ugly past and the ugly escapism have taken the whole part of you that you no longer look forward to a new beginning. Sadly, you had taken that past to be the real part of your future. What shame. Victims.

David said that he will no longer cover his sins.

> What happiness for those whose guilt has been forgiven! What joys when sins are covered over! What relief for those who have confessed their sins and God has cleared their record.
>
> There was a time when I wouldn't admit what a sinner I was. But my dishonesty made me miserable and filled my days with frustration.
>
> All day and all night your hand was heavy on me. My strength evaporated like water on a sunny day, until I finally admitted all my sins to you and stopped trying to hide them. I said to myself, "I will confess them to the Lord." And you forgave me! All my guilt is gone.
>
> Now I say that each believer should confess his sins to God when he is aware of them, while

there is time to be forgiven. Judgment will not
teach him if he does. (Psalm 32:1–6 TLB)

Jesus wants you to renounce them one by one. It could take
time. But so as not to take a toll on you, take the time to deal with
them.

There are three parts we must be fully involved in as we renounce
those pasts. Those parts are as follows:

- Your part
- Others' part
- God's part

You must be willing to repent of *your own part* and make the
necessary turnaround. Stop licking your wounds, and start lacing
your wounds—by placing your wounds before the One who would
lace it.

You must be willing to forgive others for *their parts*. The painful
memories will always come. But it is for you to "remember to forget."
Let me explain. You remember it, right? The fact that you remember it means it really exists. Then "put all your energy to forget it"
by putting it behind you and pressing on. That is what it means to
review then renounce. You must decide to renounce—and keep on
renouncing—until it loses all the power it had over you.

*If you linger too long in the valley of bitterness, pain, and weeping,
you may not get out of it. You may even be buried there as people will
dump all their trash on you.*

Mother Teresa once said, "I have found the paradox that, if I
love until it hurts, then is no more hurt, but only more love."

Lastly, accept *God's part* of complete forgiveness. He is the only
escapism you need. He is the only One your broken hearts should go.
Accept his forgiveness when he says you are forgiven.

He told the man by the pool, "You are forgiven." He told the
adulteress, "I charge you not guilty." He told Zacchaeus, "I am coming to your house." He told the criminal on the cross, "Surely today,
you will be with me in paradise."

And that settles it. What others say does not count anymore. What they announce is useless because what you renounce is what God honors. You renounce your past to reclaim your future.

When God forgives you, your case is dismissed. Accept it. Renounce it. Rise and reclaim your dominion. You see that you have a responsibility in all three parts. We must break the enemy's hold and renounce his work in our lives.

God has given us his weapons of assurance to establish this principle as you renounce your past and rise to reclaim your lost dominion.

Let's look at some of those assurances:

- His Word
- His blood
- His name

His Word

He sent His Word, and His Word heals them, and delivers them from all their sicknesses. (Psalm 107:20)

He spoke, and they were healed—snatched from the door of death. (TLB)

And I tell you this—whatever you bind on earth is bound in heaven, and whatever you free on earth will be freed in heaven. (Matthew 18:18 TLB)

One day Jesus called together his twelve apostles and gave them authority over all demons—power to cast them out—and to heal all diseases. (Luke 9:1 TLB)

And I have given you authority over all the power of the enemy, and to walk among serpents and scorpions and to crush them. Nothing shall injure you! (Luke 10:19 TLB)

Open my eyes to see wonderful things in your Word… I am completely discouraged—I lie in the dust. Revive me by your Word… May I never forget your Words, for they are my only hope… Forever, O Lord, Your Word stands firm in heaven…nothing is perfect except your Words. Oh, how I love them. I think about them all day long. They make me wiser than my enemies because they are my constant guide.

Yes, wiser than my teachers, for I am ever thinking of your rules. They make me even wiser than the aged.

I have refused to walk the paths of evil, for I will remain obedient to your Word. No, I haven't turned away from what you taught me; your Words are sweeter than honey. And since only your rules can give me wisdom and understanding, no wonder I hate every false teaching. Your Words are a flashlight to light the path ahead of me and keep me from stumbling. Psalm 119:18, 25, 43, 89, 96–105 TLB)

And you will know the truth, and the truth will set you free. (John 8:32 TLB)

I have sworn by myself, and I will never go back on my Word, for it is true—that every knee in all the world shall bow to me, and every tongue shall swear allegiance to my name. (Isaiah 45:23 TLB)

But Jesus told him, "No! For the scriptures tell us that bread won't feed men's souls: obedience to every Word of God is what we need." (Matthew 4:4 TLB)

Jesus declared, "It is written…" (Matthew 4:4, 7, 10)

And though all heaven and earth shall pass away, yet my Words remain forever true. (Luke 21:33 TLB)

Simon Peter replied, "Master, to whom shall we go? You alone have the Words that give eternal life, and we believe them and know you are the Holy Son of God." (John 6:68–69 TLB)

If ye abide in me, and my Words abide in you, ye shall ask what ye will, and it shall be done unto you. (John 15:7)

Oh, wonderful, wonderful Word of the Lord!
True wisdom its pages unfold;
And though we may read them a thousand times o'er
They never, no never grow old,
Each line hath a treasure, each promise a pearl,
That if they may secure;
And we know that when time and the world pass away,
God's Word shall forever endure.

Oh, wonderful, wonderful Word of the Lord!
The Lamp that our father above
So kindly has lighted to teach us the way
That leads to the arms of His love!
Its warnings, its counsels, are faithful and just;

Its judgments are perfect and pure,
And we know that when time and the worlds pass
away,
God's Word shall forever endure.

Oh, wonderful, wonderful Word of the Lord!
Our only salvation is there;
If carries conviction down deep in the heart,
And shows us ourselves as we are.
It tells of a Saviour, and points to the cross,
Where pardon we now may secure,
For we know that when time and the world pass
away;
God's Word shall for ever endure.

Oh, wonderful, wonderful Word of the Lord!
The hope of our friends in the past,
Its truth here so firmly they anchored their truth
Through ages eternal shall last.
Oh, wonderful, wonderful Word of the Lord!
Unchanging, abiding, and sure,
For we know that when time and the world pass
away,
God's Word shall forever endure.

—Unknown

His Blood

For God sent Christ Jesus to take the punishment for our sins and to end all God's anger against us. He used Christ's blood and our faith as the means of saving us from his wrath. In this way, he was being entirely fair, even though he did not punish those who sinned in former times. For he was looking forward to the time when Christ would come and take away those sins. (Romans 3:25 TLB)

And since by his blood he did all this for us as sinners, how much more will he do for us now that he has declared us not guilty? Now he will save us from all of God's wrath to come. (Romans 5:9 TLB)

So overflowing is his kindness toward us that he took away all our sins through the blood of His son, by whom we are saved. (Ephesians 1:7 TLB)

But now you belong to Christ Jesus, and though you once were far away from God, now you have been brought very near to him because of what Jesus Christ has done for you with his blood. (Ephesians 2:13 TLB)

And so, dear brothers, now we may walk right into the very Holy of Holies, where God is, because of the blood of Jesus. This is the fresh, new, life-giving way that Christ has opened up for us by tearing the curtain-his human body-to let us into the holy presence of God.

And since this great High Priest of ours rules over God's Household, let us go right into God himself, with true hearts fully trusting him to receive us because we have been sprinkled with Christ's blood to make us clean and because our bodies have been washed with pure water.

Now we can look forward to the salvation God has promised us. There is no longer any room for doubt, and we can tell others that salvation is ours, for there is no question that he will do what he says. (Hebrew 10:19–24 TLB)

And now may the God of peace, who brought again from the dead our Lord Jesus, equip you with all you need for doing his will. May be who became the great shepherd of the sheep by an everlasting agreement between God and you, signed with his blood, produce in you through the power of Christ all that is pleasing to him. To him be the glory forever and ever. Amen. (Hebrews 13:20 TLB)

But he paid for you with the precious life blood of Christ, the sinless, spotless Lamb of God. (1 Peter 11:19 TLB)

But, oh, how few believe it! Who will listen? To whom will God reveal his saving power? In God's eyes, he was like a tender green shoot, sprouting from a root in the dry and sterile ground. But in our eyes, there was no attractiveness at all, nothing to make us want him.

We despised him and rejected him—a man of sorrows, acquainted with bitterest grief. We turned our backs on him and looked the other way when he went by. He was despised, and we didn't care. Yet it was over grief he bore, our sorrows that weighed him down. And we thought his troubles were a punishment from God, for his own sin! But he was wounded and bruised for our sins. He was beaten that we might have peace; he was lashed—and we were healed! We—every one of us—have strayed away like sheep! We, who left God's paths to follow our own. Yet

God laid on him, the guilt and sins of every one of us! (Isaiah 53:1–6 TLB)

But if we are living in the light of God's presence, just as Christ does, then we have wonderful fellowship and joy with each other, and the blood of Jesus his Son cleanses us from every sin. (1 John 1:7 TLB)

They defeated him by the blood of the Lamb and by their testimony, for they did not love their lives, but laid them down for him. (Revelations 12:11 TLB)

In the misty days of gone,
Jesus' precious blood had pow'r
E'en the thief upon the Cross to save;
Like a bird his spirit flies
To its home in Paradise.
Thro' the pow'r of Calv'ry crimson wave.

And the blood has never lost its pow'r
No, never; no, never
Jesus blood avails for sin ever,
And will never lose its pow'r

I was lost and steep'd in guilt,
But the blood for sinners split
Washed away my sins and set me free,
Now and evermore the same,
Praise, o praise His Holy name!
Will the cleansing stream availing be.

God in mercy asks you why,
Brother sinner will you die,
When such full redemption He provides?

You have but to look and live,
Life eternal He will give,
For the pow'r of Calvary still abides.

Bring your burdens, come today,
Turn from all your sins away,
He can fully save and sanctify;
From the wrath to come now flee
Let your name recorded be
With the blood wash'd, and redeem'd on high.

—Mrs. C. H. Morris

His Name

Yet it was because of this that God raised him up to the heights of heaven and gave him a name which is above every other name, that at the name of Jesus every knee shall bow in heaven and on earth and under the earth, and every tongue shall confess that Jesus Christ is Lord to the glory of God the Father. (Philippians 2:9–11 TLB)

In solemn truth I tell you, anyone believing in me shall do the same miracles I have done, and even greater ones, because I am going to be with the Father, you can ask him for anything, using my name and I will do it, for this will bring praise to the father because of what I, the son will do for you.

Yes, ask anything using my name, and I will do it. (John 4:12–14 TLB)

You didn't choose me! I choose you! I appointed you to go and produce lovely fruit always, so that no matter what you ask for from

the father, using my name, he will give to you.
(John 15:16 TLB)

At that time you won't need to ask me for
anything, for you can go directly to the father
and ask him, and he will give you what you ask
for because you use my name.
You haven't tried this before, (but begin
now).
Ask, using my name, and you will receive,
and your cup of joy will overflow. (John 16:23–
24 TLB)

No matter what you are going through today. No matter what
you are battling with today. You can take authority over them all.
And you can rise above those ugly pasts. The first step of accomplish-
ing your victory is to know what has been done on your behalf. Jesus
had paid it all and had won the victory for you. All he needs from
you is to take the bold steps and rise to a new beginning.

However, God cannot do for you what he has given you the
power to do yourself. He said, "I have given you authority…" But
one thing the enemy doesn't want you to know is that you have the
power to restrict his movements in your life. That is why he uses
every strategy to make you remain a victim—his captive.

*Jesus had given you the authority in his name, in his blood, and in
his Word. So the court is in your ball.*

And I tell you this—whatever you bind on
earth is bound in heaven, and whatever you free
on earth will be freed in heaven. (Matthew 18:18
TLB)

These have been names that I have loved to hear,
But never has there been a name so dear
To this heart of mine, as the name Divine
The precious, precious name of Jesus.

Jesus is the sweetest name I know,
And He's just the same as His lovely name
And that's the reason why I love Him so;
Oh, Jesus is the sweetest name I know.

There is no name on earth or heaven above,
That we should give such honor and such love,
As the blessed name, let us all acclaim,
That wondrous, glorious name of Jesus.

And some day I shall see Him face to face
To thank and praise Him for His wondrous grace,
Which He gave to me, when He made me free,
The blessed Son of God called Jesus.

—Lela Long

Chapter 12

Principle Six: Rejoice in the Lord

He *rejoiced*. He found joy in the celebration.

> But his father said to the slaves, "Quick! Bring the finest robe in the house and put it on him. And a jeweled ring for his finger, and shoes! And kill the calf we have in the fattened pen. We must celebrate a feast, for this son of mine was dead and has returned to life. He was lost and I found." So the party began. (Luke 15:22–24 TLB)

This is an all-important principle that God himself demanded. However, many had failed to take this step and follow the principle. Some could not stand the ground and thus could no longer move forward in their rise to a new beginning. They had thought their powers and potentials were what brought them that far. However, God wants us to develop an attitude of gratitude and to grow in the atmosphere of praise.

Nehemiah, during the rebuilding of the wall of Jerusalem, declared, "The Joy of the Lord is my strength" (Nehemiah 8:10).

I always paraphrase it this way: "The joy of the Lord is my strength, and the strength from the Lord is my joy." I realized that I couldn't stand alone, even if I am the last man standing. There is someone standing by me and with me.

He is the One that gives me strength as I wait on him. He is the One that heals the brokenhearted and binds up their wounds. *And so in rejoicing in him, I get my strength. And in his strength, I get my joy. So I will always move on in life.*

> Always be joyful… No matter what hap-
> pens, always be thankful, for this is God's will for
> you who belong to Christ Jesus. (1 Thessalonians
> 5:16, 18 TLB)

An attitude of gratitude is the basis of all happiness.

Though it is good and healthy to always think of happy thoughts and smiles help relax muscles and reduce wrinkles, some folks may smile and not be happy. Real joy, however, comes from the heart, and it is developed in the attitude of gratitude and perfected in the atmosphere of praise.

> Always be full of joy in the Lord; I say it
> again, rejoice! (Philippians 4:4 TLB)

Read the statement again. It says, "Joy in the Lord," and not joy in any other means, not joy in some jokes, stand-up comedy, money, movies, music, sex, sports, and all other things that may only bring smiles to your face yet inside, the pains still grow in the soul.

God does have a perfect plan for your life and mine. We may look at the circumstances surrounding us and think we've been standing still forever in one painful spot. The more we pray and cry for God to help us, the more the circumstances seem to pile up.

It seems the more we pray and cry for God to take the heartache away, the more our heartbreak because God himself seems far away. The turning point cannot happen until we begin to appreciate God for who he is and praise him regardless of our situation instead of crying for him to take it all away.

Many of us tend to lose sight of the real meaning of the phrases "Praise the Lord!" or "Thank God," and we use this glibly.

According to *Webster's Dictionary*, "praise means to extol, laud, honor, acclaim, express approval. To praise, then, is to give positive affirmation, expressing our approval of something. Giving our approval means that we accept or agree with what we approve of."

To praise God for who he is means we accept and approve him of who he is and approve of his ways, which are always beyond our reasoning.

> This plan of mine is not what you would work out, neither are my thoughts the same as yours! For just as the heavens are higher than the earth, so are my ways higher than yours, and my thoughts than yours. (Isaiah 55:8–9 TLB)

To praise God in difficult situations, heartbreaks, victimizations, disappointments, and sickness means literally that we accept and approve of its happenings as part of God's plan for our lives and that he will make all things work for good in our lives (Romans 8:28).

We can't really praise God without being thankful for the things we are praising him for. And we can't really be thankful without being happy about whatever we are thankful for. Praising then involves both gratitude and joy.

The very fact that we praise God and not some unknown fate also means that we are accepting the fact that God is aware of what is happening. And no matter how we caused it or permitted it to happen in our lives, God will surely work it out for good. Otherwise, it would make no sense to thank God for it (1 Thessalonians 5:16–18).

I have met quite a few folks who are able to praise God for their circumstances, simply because they accept the word of the Bible that they are to rejoice and praise God for everything. Praising God, they soon experience the results of an attitude of consistent thanksgiving and joy, and in turn, their faith is strengthened, and they can continue to live with the joy of the Lord as their strength.

"The joy of the Lord is my strength. And the strength from the Lord is my joy."

Someone had once said, "I just don't understand. I try praising God, but it is so hard for me to believe that he really has a hand in all the horrible things that have happened to me lately."

We say we don't understand, and some of us get stuck right there. Our understanding becomes a real stumbling block in our relationship with God. God, however, has a perfect plan for our understanding, and when we use it his way, it isn't a stumbling block but a stepping-stone—a wonderful aid to our faith and a booster for our strength.

Have you got to ask why would a great famine arise after this young man had wasted his inheritance? Was the famine a stimulant that would make him get to his senses? Your answer is as good as mine.

However, we're not supposed to push our understanding out of the way, grit our teeth, and say, "It doesn't make sense to me, but I'll praise the Lord if it kills me and if that's the only way I can get out of this mess."

Hello, that's not praising. That's manipulating! We've all tried to manipulate God, and it is wonderful to know that he loves us too much to let us get away with it.

We are to praise God with our understanding, not despite it. The Book of Psalms opens our eyes to this fact. The writers were not just praising God as a means of manipulation but out of understanding and appreciation.

Our understanding gets us into trouble when we try to figure out *why* and *how* God brings certain circumstances into our lives. We can never understand *why* and *how* God does some things, but he wants us to accept with our understanding that he does it.

> For I know the plans I have for you, says
> the Lord. They are plans for good and not evil,

to give you a future and a hope. (Jeremiah 29:11
TLB)

This is the basis of our praise. God wants you to understand
that he loves you and that he has a plan for you. Despite how badly
you might have offended him and others, God wants you to understand that he still loves you and has a plan for you. Despite how badly
you might have been hurt, rejected, disappointed, and heartbroken,
God wants you to understand that he still loves you and has a plan
for you.

> And we know that all that happens to us
> is working for our good if we love God and are
> fitting into His plans. (Romans 8:28 TLB)

He said that his plan is not for you to work out but for him to
work out. He knows the end even before the beginning began. And
he knows how to make it work out for good. All he needs to make
this happen is you.

Are you surrounded by difficult circumstances right now? Have
you been struggling to understand why they have come to you? Are
you battling with an ugly past that has left a terrible scar? Are you
being haunted by your actions? Are you heartbroken and seemingly
to ask, "why me?" Then try to accept with your understanding that
God does love you and has allowed those circumstances because he
knows they are good for you. Praise him for what he has brought into
your life; do it deliberately and with your understanding.

Paul said, "I will sing in the spirit, and I will sing with understanding." (1 Corinthians 14:15).

When you are in the center of God-given purpose, you can
always smile in the storm because you know—and understand—
that God is working it out for your good, and you are coming out
strong into a new beginning. This will change your focus from what's

impossible to what's possible. It will also turn your attention from the scars to the stars.

> No matter what happens, always be thankful, for this is God's will for you who belong to Christ Jesus. (1 Thessalonians 5:18 TLB)

When you develop this attitude, it becomes part of you. You will stand strong, and the power of the past will be broken.

> Praise the Lord! Yes, really praise Him!
> I will praise him as long as I live, yes, even with my dying breath.
> Don't look to men for help, their greatest leaders fail, for every man must die. His breathing stops, life ends, and in a moment all he planned for himself is ended.
> But happy is the man who has the God of Jacob as his helper, whose hope is in the Lord his God—the God who made both earth and heaven, the seas and everything in them.
> He is the God who keeps every promise, who gives justice to the poor and oppressed and food to the hungry.
> He frees the prisoners and opens the eyes of the blind; he lifts the burdens from those bent down beneath their loads. For the Lord loves good men. He protects the immigrants and cares for the orphans and widows. But he turns topsy-turvy the plans of the wicked.
> The Lord will reign forever. O Jerusalem, your God is king in every generation! Halleluiah! Praise the Lord! (Psalm 146 TLB)

CHAPTER 13

PRINCIPLE SEVEN: REPEAT WHAT GOD HAD SAID ABOUT YOU

He *repeated* what his father said about him.

> But his father said to the servants, "Quick! Bring the finest robe in the house and put it on him. Get a ring for his finger and sandals for his feet. And kill the calf we have been fattening. We must celebrate with a feast, for this son of mine was dead and has now returned to life. He was lost, but now he is found." So, the party began. (Luke 15:22–24 NLT)

Whatever opinion others have about him doesn't matter. Whatever God said he is, that he is. When God says, "Yes," to your case, other people's contrary opinion is their own problem.

Meanwhile, the older son was out in the fields working. When he returned home, he heard dance music coming from the house, and he asked one of the servants what was going on.

"Your brother is back"; he was told, "and your father has killed the calf we were fattening and has prepared a great feast to celebrate his coming home again unharmed."

The older brother was angry and wouldn't go in. His father came out and begged him, but he replied, "All these years I've worked hard for you and never once refused to do a single thing you told me to, and in all that time you never gave me even one young goat for a feast with my friends. Yet when this son of yours comes back after spending your money on prostitutes, you celebrate by killing the finest calf we have on the place."

"Look, dear son," his father said to him, "you and I are very close, and everything I have is yours. But it is right to celebrate. For he is your brother, and he was dead and has come back to life! He was lost and is found!" (Luke 15: 25–32 TLB)

Having now understood that God has a plan for you no matter what you might have passed through, you must now line up your words with God's words. People might have known your past and could tell how your future would be, but it is what God says about you that really matters.

Words are powerful—they either build you up or pull you down. They serve either as a projection or as a limitation. That is why you must make God's words your words too.

To rise into a new beginning of victorious living, you must begin to say what God says, regardless of your past and the situation you presently find yourself in. When you say anything contrary, you're putting yourself in disagreement with him.

No matter what people say around you, you are what God says you are. No matter what your past is revealing about you, you are what God says you are. No matter what events and circumstances around are depicting, you are what God says you are. No matter what is going on and if it seems there is no hope, you are what God says you are.

You are what God says you are. If anyone disagrees, that's their problem.

Other people's opinions about you should not be your own business but their own business, and it is impolite if you do not let them mind their business. What should be your own business is what God had said about you.

When you've got God's verdict about your life, others' opinions do not count at all. God's opinion of you is the only solid and enduring foundation to build your self-worth and self-esteem. God's verdict of you is found in his Word.

When he says, "You're free," you are free indeed. When he says, "You're forgiven," you are forgiven indeed. When he says, "You're healed," you are healed indeed. When he says, "Rise up!" rise up! When he says, "Let the party begin!" go ahead, rise to reclaim your dominion, and celebrate.

Build your life around what God says about you, and fill your thoughts and talks with it. Whether you are struggling or soaring, stand on the promises of God.

If only you know how God feels about you, you would not be so critical of yourself or so conscious of the opinions of others. God had known you right before you were born. He is the only one who knows how you came into being and the only one that can determine how you will be.

Do not let those who never knew how you were formed deter-mine how you could live. Do not let those who never knew how you were made determine how you could make it in life.

> You made all the delicate, inner parts of my body and knit them together in my mother's womb.
>
> Thank you for making me so wonderfully complex! It is amazing to think about. Your workmanship is marvelous—and how well I know it. You were there while I was being formed in utter seclusion! You saw me before I was born and scheduled each day of my life before I began to breathe. Every day was recorded in your book!
>
> How precious it is, Lord, to realize that you are thinking about me constantly! I can't even count how many times a day your thoughts turn toward me. And when I waken in the morning, you are still thinking of me! (Psalm 139:13–18 TLB)

You should stop running from place to place looking for love and security. When they break your heart, where would you go? However, when you open your heart to God, he will speak his word into your life and make you see who he wants you to be.

Listen to what God says about you as you apply this principle to your life:

> The high and lofty One who inhabits eter-nity, the Holy One, says this: "I live in that high and holy place where those with contrite, humble spirits dwell, and I refresh the humble and give new courage to those with repentant hearts... I have seen what they do, but I will heal them any-way! I will lead them and comfort them, helping them to mourn and to confess their sins. Peace,

peace to them, both near and far, for I will heal them all." (Isaiah 57:15–19 TLB)

Whenever you feel downcast, go back to his Word, and see what God has to say about you. There's nothing compared to God's love for you. No matter what opinion others have about you, if God is on your side, their opinions don't count.

All you need to do is to always repeat what God says about you, and you will always rise to a new beginning.

Let us look at the Word of God. This is the testimony of Apostle Paul:

> For from the beginning, God decided that those who came to him—and all along he who would—should become like his Son, so that his son would be the first, with many brothers.
>
> And having chosen us, he called us to come to him, and when we came, he declared us "not guilty," filled us his glory.
>
> What can we ever say to such wonderful things as these? If God is on our side, who can ever be against us? Since he did not spare even his own Son for us but gave him up for us all, won't he also surely give us everything else?
>
> Who dares accuse us whom God has chosen for his own? Will God? No! He is the one who has forgiven us and given us the right standing with himself.
>
> Who then will condemn us? Will Christ? No! For he is the one who died for us and came back to life again for us and is sitting at the place of highest honor next to God, pleading for us there in heaven.
>
> Who then can ever keep Christ's love from us? When we have trouble or calamity, when we are haunted down or destroyed, is it because he

doesn't love us anymore? And if we are hungry or penniless or in danger or threatened with death, has God deserted us?

No, for the scriptures tell us that for his sake we must be ready to face death at every moment of the day—we are like sheep awaiting slaughter, but despite all this, overwhelming victory is ours through Christ who loved us enough to die for us.

For I am convinced that nothing can ever separate us from his love.

Death can't, and life can't. The angels won't, and all the powers of hells itself cannot keep God's love away.

Our fears for today, our worries about tomorrow, or where we are-high above the sky, or in the deepest ocean—nothing will ever be able to separate us from the love of God demonstrated by our Lord Jesus Christ when he died for us. (Romans 8:29–39 TLB)

Rejoice in the Lord! Oh, let His mercy cheer,
He sunders the bands that enthrall,
Redeem'd by His blood why should we ever fear?
Since Jesus is our "all in all"?

If God be for us, if God be for us,
If God be for us,
Who can be against us? Who? Who? Who?
Who can be against us, against us?

Be strong in the Lord! Rejoicing in His might,
Be loyal and true day by day,
When evils assail, be valiant for the right,
And He will be our strength and stay

LET THE PARTY BEGIN!

Confide in His word His promises so sure
In Christ they are "yeah and Amen."
Though earth pass away, they ever shall endure,
'Tis written o'er and o'er again

Abide in the Lord secure in His control,
'Tis life everlasting begun
To pluck from His hand the weakest, trembling soul
It never, never can be done!

—James McGranahan

Chapter 14

Principle Eight: Reclaim Your Restoration and Receive Your Revival

He was *restored* and *revived*, and he *reclaimed* his lost dominion.

> But his father said to the slaves, "Quick! Bring the finest robe in the house and put it on him. And a jeweled ring for his finger, and shoes! And kill the calf we have in the fattened pen. We must celebrate with a feast, for this son of mine was dead and has returned to life. He was lost and is found." So, the party began.
>
> "It is right to celebrate…for he was dead and has come back to life! He was lost and is found!" (Luke 15:22–25, 32 TLB)

This is the last principle that will put you on the platform of a new beginning. This is the step to fulfillment. It is the principle of *restoration*. This is the principle of *recovery*. This is the step toward *revival*. This is the principle that you apply to *receive your restoration and reclaim your dominion.*

Those lost years were restored for the prodigal son. He had a new beginning. Everything in his past now became "once upon a time." God wants you to "do the things you did at first" (Revelations 2:5).

Make a list of the things you used to do when the relationship was great, and begin to do them again. Do not wait till you feel like it. Just keep doing it. Keep doing it till you feel it, till the joy of your first love reignites.

You can start your life over again. You can dream again. You can live again. But remember, it all started with the first principle—*remember*!

> Fear not my people; be glad now and rejoice, for he has done amazing things for you. Let the flocks and herds forget their hunger; the pastures will turn green again. The trees will bear their fruit; the fig tree and grapevines will flourish once more.
>
> Rejoice, O people of Jerusalem, Rejoice in the Lord your God! For the rains he sends are token of forgiveness. Once more the autumn rain will come, as well as those of spring. The threshing floors will pile high again with wheat, and the presses overflow with olive oil and wine.
>
> And I will give you back the crops the locust ate!—My great destroying army that I sent against you. Once again you will have all the food you want.
>
> Praise the Lord, who does these miracles for you. Never again will my people experience a disaster such as this. And you will know that I am here among my people shall never again be dealt a blow like this. After I have poured out my rains again, I will pour out my Spirit upon all of you! Your sons and daughters will prophesy; your

old men will dream dreams, and your young men
see visions.

And I will pour out my Spirit even on your
slaves, men and women alike. (Joel 2:21–29
TLB)

God says, "I will restore to you the years…" (Joel 2:25)—those
years you lived like a victim, those periods you were brokenhearted.
God says that he will restore them all to you.

God is saying, "As you take this final step and apply this last
principle, I will give you a new beginning. I will give you new relationships. I will give you new opportunities. I will give you new
ground. I will give you new hope. I will give you a new life. Old
things will be part of your history. And new things will be part of
your story. For every new beginning, there is always a once upon a
time. And I will give you a new beginning."

Revival is eminent in your rise to a new beginning. God wants to
restore you to that relationship he once had with you—even beyond
that level. All you need to do is to *receive and reclaim it.*

And so the party began. He stepped up and rose to a new
beginning. Old things passed away, and everything became new (2
Corinthians 5:17). The party began for this young man, and everything became new. He was even restored far beyond where he'd
thought. And that was what God meant when he declared, "Rise up."
The first principle is the most important, but you must complete it
all, taking it one step at a time.

Myles Monroe said, "There is something for you to start that is
destined for you to finish."

The Psalmist declared the following:

> Turn us again to yourself, O God, Look
> from on us in joy and love, only then shall we
> be saved.
>
> Turn us again to yourself, O God of Hosts,
> Look down on us joy and love, only then shall
> we be saved.

> Strengthen the man you love, the son of
> your choice, and we will never forsake you again.
> Revive us to trust in you.
>
> Turn us again to yourself, O God of the
> armies of Heaven. Look down on us, your face
> aglow with joy and love-only then shall we be
> saved. (Psalm 80:3, 7, 17–19 TLB)

> Oh, revive us! Then your people can rejoice
> in you again. (Psalm 85:6 TLB)

No matter how bad you might have fallen, God still has a purpose for you, and he still believes in you. No matter what you might have lost, God still has a purpose for you, and he still believes in you. No matter how heartbroken you might have been, God still has a purpose for you and still believes in you.

No matter how lonely you might have been, God still has a purpose for you and still believes in you. No matter how long you have been a victim, God still has a purpose for you and still believes in you.

No matter how deeply you might have been hurt and wounded, God still has a purpose for you and still believes in you. No matter how unforgiven people have regarded you, God still has a purpose for you and still believes in you.

God wants you to rise into a new beginning because he loves you and still believes in you. If you still have that life in you, you can rise to a new beginning.

Bob Gass said, "It's not what you have lost, but what you have left that counts."

And Robert Schuller added, "Look at what you have left, never look at what you have lost."

This is the summation of Jeremiah on this matter:

> O Lord, all peace and all prosperity have
> long since gone, for you have taken them away.
> I have forgotten what enjoyment is. All hope is

gone; my strength has turned to water, for the Lord has left me.

Oh, remember the bitterness and suffering you have dealt to me!

For I can never forget these awful years; always my soul will live in utter shame.

Yet there is one ray of hope: his compassion never ends.

It is only the Lord's mercies that have kept us from complete destruction. Great is his faithfulness, his loving-kindness begins afresh each day.

My soul claims the Lord as my inheritance; therefore I will hope in him. (Lamentation 3:17–24 TLB)

There is hope for you—hope to take those steps, hope to live again, hope to rise to a new beginning, the hope of a new life.

Turn thou us unto thee, O Lord, and we shall be turned, renew our days as of old. (Lamentation 5:21)

Turn us around and bring us back to you again! That is our only hope! Give us back the joys we used to have! (TLB)

Your recovery is your responsibility. Rise up to a new life. Rise and reclaim your dominion. Let the party begin.

Revive Thy work, O Lord!
Thy mighty arm make bare;
Speak with the voice that wakes the dead,
And make Thy people hear!

Revive Thy work, O Lord,
While here to thee we blow;
Descend, o gracious Lord descend,
Oh, come and bless us now.

Revive Thy work, o Lord!
Disturb this sleep of death;
Quicken the smould'ning embers now
By Thine Almighty breath.

Revive Thy work, O Lord!
Create soul thirst for thee;
And hung' ring for the bread of life,
Oh, may our spirits be!

Revive Thy work, O Lord!
Exalt Thy precious name;
And by the Holy Ghost, our love;
For Thee and Thine aflame.

—Albert Midlane

Rise from your ugly past and horrible present. Rise into the glory of God. Rise from your barrenness and unproductively. Rise into fruitfulness and multiplication. Rise from your ridicules. Rise into your miracles. Rise from your humiliation. Rise into exaltation. Rise from your poverty. Rise into prosperity. Rise from failure. Rise into success.

Rise from rejection and dejection. Rise into celebration. Rise from the miry clay. Rise onto the solid rock. Rise from death. Rise into life. Rise from the darkness. Rise into the light. Rise from helplessness and hopelessness. Rise into being a helper and hope for others. Rise from impotence. Rise into importance.

Jesus has come into your rescue, and he is saying, "Rise."

So NOW, *in Jesus's name, I decree, and I declare, "You shall* RISE! AMEN*!"*

> Arise, Shine, for thy light is come and the glory of the Lord is risen upon thee. (Isaiah 60:1)

> For your shame, ye shall have double and for confusion, they shall rejoice in their portion therefore in their land they shall possess the double everlasting joy shall be onto them. (Isaiah 61:7)

As you rise, take up your bed, and walk straight home. As you rise, return to the place of your dominion. You are no longer the helpless and hopeless looking for any help even it means an abomination, but you have become the help of the helpless and hope of the hopeless because as you rise, you are now a solution to somebody's problem.

As you rise, you now have a vision with a mission. As you rise, you are shining. He shall give you rest from all your troubles, pains, and worries. He only has that rest. Read Matthew 11:28–30.

> *My heart was distressed neath Jehovah's dread frown,*
> *And low in the pit where my sins dragged me down,*
> *I cried to the Lord from the deep miry clay,*
> *Who tenderly brought me out to golden day.*
>
> *He bro't me out of the miry clay,*
> *He set my feet on the Rock to stay;*
> *He puts a song in my soul today,*
> *A song of praise, hallelujah!*
>
> *He placed me upon the strong Rock by His side,*
> *My steps were established and here I'll abide,*
> *No danger of falling while here I remain,*
> *But stand by his grace until the crown I gain.*

He gave me a song, 'twas a new song of praise,
By day and by night its sweet notes I will raise,
My heart's overflowing; I'm happy and free,
I'll praise my Redeemer, who has rescued me.

I'll sing of His wonderful mercy to me,
I'll praise Him till all men His goodness shall see,
I'll sing of salvation at home and abroad,
Till many shall hear the truth and trust in God.

I'll tell of the pit with its gloom and despair,
I'll praise the dear father who answered my prayer,
I'll sing my new song, the glad story of love,
Then join in the chorus with the saints above.

—Henry J. Zelley

I rise over every oppression, compression, suppression, and intimi-
dation. I rise into my dominion in Jesus's name.

CHAPTER 15

TAKE YOUR STAND IN THE LORD

> Arise, shine; for thy light is come, and the glory of the LORD is risen upon thee. For, behold, the darkness shall cover the earth, and gross darkness the people: but the LORD shall arise upon thee, and his glory shall be seen upon thee. And the Gentiles shall come to thy light, and kings to the brightness of thy rising. (Isaiah 60:1–3)

Let me point it straight to you that these principles may be difficult to apply and the most difficult grounds to stand on. This is because there are going to be a lot of pressures coming your way to make you back out.

As you apply these principles for a new beginning, your responsibility is most needed to reclaim your lost dominion. This is where you play your part and stand your ground. You cannot do it alone though, but it all depends on you.

Let's look at five things you must do to stand your ground as you take this step to press on to higher grounds:

- Be deeply rooted in God's Word.
- Develop the habit of prayer.

- Destroy the link to your past.
- Wait upon the Lord.
- Let the party begin.

I'm pressing on the upward way,
New heights I'm gaining every day;
Still praying as I'm onward bound,
"Lord, plant my feet on higher ground."

Lord, lift me up and let me stand,
By faith, on Heaven's tableland,
A higher plane than I have found;
Lord, plant my feet on higher ground.

My heart has no desire to stay
Where doubts arise and fears dismay;
Though some may dwell where those abound,
My prayer, my aim, is higher ground.

I want to live above the world,
Though Satan's darts at me are hurled;
For faith has caught the joyful sound,
The song of saints on higher ground.

I want to scale the utmost height
And catch a gleam of glory bright;
But still I'll pray till heav'n I've found,
"Lord, plant my feet on higher ground."

—Johnson Oatman Jr.

Be Deeply Rooted in God's Word

The Word of God is the only solid and strong foundation to stand on. The Word of God holds you firm, and when you hold on to it, nothing can shake you off.

> And now just as you trusted Christ to save you, trust him, too, for each day's problems; live in vital union with him.
>
> Let your roots grow down into him and draw up nourishment from him. See that you go on growing in the Lord and become strong and vigorous in the truth you were taught. Let your lives overflow with joy and thanksgiving for all he has done.
>
> Don't let others spoil your faith and joy with their philosophies, their wrong and shallow answers built on men's thoughts and ideas, instead of on what Christ has said. (Colossians 2:6–8 TLB)

God has given his Word to sustain you and make you stand strong and upright. In Mathew 4:4–11, when the devil came to tempt Jesus, Jesus was ready with his answers. Three times, the tempter tried to get Jesus to submit to his suggestions using the Scripture to want to confuse Jesus, but each time, Jesus responded with the same Scripture saying, "It is written."

When the enemy tries to plant his thoughts and suggestions in your mind, have your "It is written" ready. Build yourself up in the Word of God. Be on the alert so as not to be caught off guard. God's Word is sure and true. His promises are there for you to guide and to guard. When you are deeply rooted in God's Word, you will be able to stand strong in the world.

Standing on the promises of Christ my King,
Thro eternal ages let His praises ring;

Glory in the highest, I will shout and sing,
Standing on the promises of God.

Standing, standing
Standing on the promises of God my Savior,
Standing, standing,
I'm standing on the promises of God.

Standing on the promises that cannot fail,
Where the howling storms of doubt and fear assail
By the Living Word of God I shall prevail,
Standing on the promises of God.

Standing on the promises of Christ the Lord,
Bound to Him eternally by love's strong cord,
Overcoming daily with the spirit's sword,
Standing on the promises of God.

Standing on the promises I cannot fall,
List'ning every moment to the spirit call,
Resting in my Savior as my all in all,
Standing on the promises of God.

—R. Kelso Carter

Develop the Habit of Prayer

Jesus told his disciples, "Keep alert and pray. Otherwise, the temptation will overpower you. For the spirit indeed is willing, but how weak the body is!" (Matthew 26:41 TLB).

Your old nature should always be taken to the place of prayer. You may have a strong and willing spirit, but unless you develop the habit of prayer, your weak flesh and emotions can take control of your life.

The most effective weapon the enemy has against you is you.

The devil cannot get you without your approval of him. And to get you down and out, he will always target the weak part of painful memories of the past—in your emotions.

In prayer, however, you present yourself to God. As you spend time in God's presence, you see yourself as he sees you, not as you are seeing yourself or as the world is seeing you. You may be seeing yourself as a victim. The world may be seeing you as a victim, but God is seeing you as a victor that needs to rise above the pain and the shame.

Prayer is not always the place of warfare. Prayer is always the place of communion and communication. Prayer is the place of healing and filling. Prayer is the place of connecting with God, not just confronting the enemies. Prayer is not just a place to fight but also a place to hide.

It is in the place of prayer that you pour out your heart to God, and he heals your broken heart and binds up your wounds.

It is in the place of prayers that the healings take place. That is where you tell God all your troubles and let him heal you in his own way and not your own way.

It is in the place of prayer that your peace of mind is restored. You will have the courage to dream again. You will develop the ability to love and be loved in a healthy way. And you will have the strength, boldness, and courage to say, "No," to every means the devil will want to use to get you down and out.

God can break every chain that links you to the past. He can wipe the slate clean of the mistakes you've ever made. He can restore everything that has been taken from you.

You may think you have a strong spirit to fight on, but the enemy knows your weakness. Your wounds have been exposed to him. And that is the entire target he needs. But you cannot fight alone. You cannot stand alone. There is a place to hand over everything to Jesus. There is a place to stand and be assured that Jesus is standing with you. And that is the place of prayer.

> Don't worry about anything, instead, pray
> about everything; tell God your needs, and don't
> forget to thank him for his answers. If you do

this, you will experience God's peace, which is far more wonderful than the human mind can understand. His peace will keep your hearts quiet and at rest as you trust in Christ Jesus. (Philippians 4:6–7 TLB)

I must tell Jesus all of my trials
I cannot bear these burdens alone;
In my distress, He kindly will help me,
He ever loves and cares for His own.

I must tell Jesus! I must tell Jesus!
I cannot bear my burdens alone;
I must tell Jesus! I must tell Jesus!
Jesus can help me, Jesus alone.

I must tell Jesus all of my troubles,
He is a kind, compassionate friend,
If I but ask Him, He will deliver
Make of my troubles quickly an end.

O how the world to evil allures me!
O how my heart is tempted to sin!
I must tell Jesus, and He will help me
Over the world the vict'ry to win.

—Elisha A. Hoffman

Destroy the Link with Your Past

A bridge serves as a link, a means of access to a place because a gap has been created. It is for you to burn those bridges that you have crossed behind you.

Don't put yourself in the position that gives your past access to your future and ruin life again.

Any bridge to the past that refuses to burn just gives the enemy an invitation and an entry point back into your life.

When God took Israel out of Egypt, they passed through the Red Sea. God then directed Moses after they've reached the other side to stretch out his rod to close the parted Red Sea. The Egyptian army that wanted to catch up with them all drowned in the Red Sea.

However, more than once, the children of Israel wanted to go back to Egypt but never knew how. Why? The sea that served as the bridge away from their past had been burnt so that it will not also serve as the bridge for their past to catch up with them nor for them to turn back to their past. Remember, it was that the Red Sea that they crossed to overcome their pasts and move to a better future. That same Red Sea could serve as the link back to their pasts if not taken care of.

Bridges, we all have them. This one that I am talking about is that which serves as a link, access, or route to a beautiful and glorious future, as well as access back to that ugly past. They are in our thoughts, talks, actions, and reactions, even interactions. They are in the books we read, the friends we keep, the movies we watch, and what we think of ourselves.

Bridges of corrupt friends, pornography, addiction, and every other thing associated with immorality that had once made us lose our dominion and become victims need to be burned. Bridges of unforgiveness, bitterness, anger, envy that you have crossed to start over a new life all need to be destroyed.

We have crossed the bridges to overcome those ugly pasts; going back to the ugly pasts would mean we are crossing the bridges back. We should not give the devil another chance to get us down and out.

A bridge must be crossed once to move ahead in life. When you cross it again, it means your life is going in circles, and that is not a sign of progress but regress.

You have heard people say this, "Be nice to the people you meet on your way up because you will still meet them on your way down." I believe this is not only a very wrong perspective of life but also a dangerous principle of life. There are things wrong with this kind of statement, and we need to address them:

- You are on your way up, and you met people on your way up. It means they are also on their way up. To still meet them on your way down means you expect them also to go down as you are going down.
- You are on your way up. Do not expect to meet the same people on your way down that you met on your way up. It means you expect them to be stuck or stagnant and that you will meet them the way you left them.
- You are on your way up. You should not expect yourself to someday be on your way down. The old hymn says, "A higher plain than I have found, Lord, plant my feet on higher ground." David prayed to God, "When my heart is overwhelmed. Lead me to the Rock that is higher than I" (Psalm 61:1–2). Where do you put these in this principle?
- You are on your way up. Expect to see others on their way up too. Give a hand to those you meet on your way up; you may need their hands to either pull you up or push you up when you are in your down moments too.
- You are on your way up. You are expected to make progress, not regress. So why should you expect yourself to be on your way down someday, somehow?
- You are on your way up. You are expected to be nice to those you meet on your way up because you may never meet them again. You will leave a great impression on their hearts about you and about life. With that, you have made an impact on your way up and not just when you get there.
- You are on your way up. You are expected to pull or push other people up too. And if you cannot do that for them, you are expected to influence them to the way up and not allow them to pull you down.

If you want to get it well, it should have been, "Be nice to the people you meet on your way down. You may meet them again on your way up," and not the other way round. Although such is life, it is also a wrong approach to life.

You should not expect to meet the same people on your way down but on your way up. Several people will come your way—either up or down. However, the best way to go is up, not down and not in a circle.

So instead of applying this wrong principle to life, I would advise you to follow this principle:

> Be nice to the people you meet on your way up. You might need them along the way or meet them again on your way up. You might even meet some other people on a higher ground who might have seen what you did to the people on your way up.

Circular motion is in no specific direction. There is a difference between motion and direction. You must not confuse motion with direction. A direction is a motion with a notion. The Israelites crossed the Red Sea once. They crossed the Jordan River once. The wall of Jericho fell once. They only needed one experience of overcoming a particular past at a time.

Every bridge crossed brought about a new experience. When an ugly situation is repeating, it shows that the bridge has not been destroyed and the people are just crossing back and forth. And the song the people sing will always be, "We've passed through this road before, and we are sure to pass through it again."

The Israelites also experienced this situation when they moved in circles around a particular mountain. And the Lord had to intervene. God told Moses, "You have moved around this mountain long enough. Move forward."

> Then we turned and took our journey into
> the wilderness by the way of the Red sea, as the
> Lord spake unto me: and we compassed mount
> Seir many days.

And the Lord spake unto me, saying, "Ye have compassed this mountain long enough: turn you northward." (Deuteronomy 2:1–3)

Then we turned back across the wilderness toward the Red Sea, for so the Lord had instructed me. For many years we wandered around the area of Mount Seir. Then at last the Lord said, "You have stayed here long enough. Turn northward." (TLB)

Many folks do experience this roller-coaster lifestyle. One day, they are up, and it seems they had overcome the ugly past. The next day, they are down because the past just couldn't go off, only to be up again and then down again.

It just keeps on going and coming like a roller coaster. It means something is still connecting them to the past they had overcome, and that was the same bridge they had crossed to overcome that past. This is not the picture of a life in progress.

Just like the Israelites, many folks today still move in circles. They have the same ugly past, crossed the bridge to overcome the past, and then crossed back the bridge to get back to the past, only to cross it again to overcome the past, and it goes on and on.

They have the same problem and the same solution over again. And it goes on for years. It seems they are making progress, but they are only moving in circles. God said, "You must 'move forward.'" *Let your motion become direction.*

It may not be that easy breaking with the past though because of the familiar terrain. But when you put in all your efforts to break with the past, the Lord will always be there to strengthen you and make you move forward without checking back on the bridge you had crossed but always on the lookout for new challenges to overcome.

The devil will not be happy with you and would always rouse up some opposition to pressurize you to make you change your mind and take a look back at your past and long for a way back. But when you have burned or broken the bridge, there will not be any link to take you back to your past.

When salvation came to the people in Ephesus, the new Christians in the city brought out all their idols, old books of witchcraft, pornographic images, and everything associated with their past and burned them publicly in the town square. When they did, a riot broke out because the devil was not happy, so he stirred up some opposition. But God was there to see them through.

> The story of what happened spread quickly all through Ephesus, to Jews and Greeks alike, and a solemn fear descended on the city, and the name of the Lord Jesus was greatly honored. Many of the believers who had been practicing black magic confessed their deeds and brought their incantation books and charms and burned them at a public bonfire.
>
> (Someone estimated the value of the books at $10,000). This indicates how deeply the whole area was stirred by God's message…
>
> But about that time, a big blowing up developed in Ephesus concerning the Christians. It began with Demetrius, a silversmith who employed many craftsmen to manufacture silver shrines of the Greek goddess Diana. He called a meeting of his men, together with others employed in related trades, and addressed them as follows:
>
> "Gentlemen, this business is our income. As you know so well from what you've seen and heard, this man Paul has persuaded many, many people that handmade gods aren't gods at all. As a result, our sales volume is going down! And this trend is evident not only here in Ephesus, but throughout the entire province! Of course, I am not only talking about the business aspect of this

situation and our loss of income, but also of the possibility that the temple of the great goddess Diana will lose its influence, and that Dianathis magnificent goddess worshipped not only throughout this part of Turkey but all around the world—will be forgotten!" At this their anger boiled and they began shouting, "Great is Diana of the Ephesus!"

A crowd began to gather, and soon the city was filled with confusion. Everyone rushed to the amphitheater, dragging along Gaius and Aristarchus, Paul's traveling companions, for trial. (Acts 19:17–35 TLB)

Read the rest of the story in Acts 19:36–41. The enemy feared losing his victims, so he would always raise opposition. God is, however, always there to help you out. You must also "make no room for the flesh, to fulfill the lust thereof" (Romans 13:14).

In burning those bridges, you must not look back. Smash the rearview mirror, and move forward. Let your thoughts be on what you are going to become and not what has happened to you.

Finally, brethren, whatsoever things are true, whatsoever things are honest, whatsoever things are just, whatsoever things are pure, whatsoever things are lovely, whatsoever things are of good report if there be any virtue, and if there be any praise, think on these things. (Philippians 4:8)

Wait upon the Lord

Learn to rest on the Lord and replenish your strength in him. He is the only one that can give you the much-needed strength when you learn to wait upon him. You learn to have patience in allowing God to deal with you and your past.

It has to do with the issue of the heart. Having an open-heart surgery, even a heart transplant, is never a hasty case. It takes total care and carefulness. It takes total surrender, submission, and yielding. It is not what you can do on your own. It is what God can do for you. And you must allow God to do it his own way—his own period and pace. That is when his strength can only come out in your own weakness.

> When you came to Christ, he sets you free from your evil desires, not by a bodily operation of circumcision but by a spiritual operation, the baptism of your souls. For in baptism, you see how your old, evil nature died with him and was buried with him, and then you came up out of death with him and war buried with him, and then you came up out of death with him into a new life because you trusted the word of the mighty God who raised Christ from the dead.
>
> You were dead in sins, and your sinful desires were not yet cut away. Then he gave you a share in the very life of Christ, for he forgave all your sins, and blotted out the charges proved against you, and list of his commandments, which you had not obeyed. He took this list of sins and destroyed if by nailing it to Christ's cross.
>
> In this way God took away Satan's power to accuse you of sin, and God openly displayed to the whole Christ's triumph at the cross where your sins were all taken away. (Colossians 2:11–15 TLB)

Whenever you let go, you let God. He will fight for you and stand by you. When you wait on him, you will not rush out till he is through with you.

> O Jacob, O Israel, how can you say that the Lord doesn't see your troubles and isn't being

fair? Don't you yet understand? Don't you know by now that the everlasting God, the creator of the farthest parts of the earth, never grows faint or weary? No one can fathom the depths of his understanding.

He gives power to the tired and worn out, and strength to the weak. Even youths shall be exhausted, and the young men will all give up. But they that wait upon the Lord shall renew their strength. They shall mount up with wings like eagles; they shall run and not be weary; they shall walk and not faint. (Isaiah 40:27–31 TLB)

Day by Day and with each passing moment,
Strength I find to meet my trials here,
Trusting in my father's wise bestowment,
I've no cause for worry or for fear.
He whose heart is kind beyond all measure
Gives unto each day what he deems best
Lovingly its part of pain and pleasure,
Mingling toil with peace and rest.

Ev'ry day the Lord Himself is near me
With a special mercy for each hour,
All my cares He fail would bear, and cheer me,
He whose name is counselor and pow'r.
The protection of His child and treasure
Is a charge that on Himself He laid;
"As your days your strength shall be in measure,"
This is the pledge to me He made.

Help me then in ev'ry tribulation
So to trust your promises, o Lord,
That I lose not faith's sweet consolation
Offered me within your holy word.
Help me, Lord, when toil and trouble meeting,

E'er to take, as from a father's hand,
One by one, the days, the moments fleeting
Till I reach the Promised Land.

—Carolina Sandell Berg

Let the Party Begin

The world is waiting for your dominion. God has created you for dominion. You might have lost it, but God has told you that you can reclaim it. You might have yet to discover it, but God has assured you that you have been created for dominion. There is a party waiting for you as the main celebrant.

> The older brother was angry and wouldn't go in. His father came out and begged him, but he replied, "All these years I've slaved for you and never once refused to do a single thing you told me to. And in all that time you never gave me even one young goat for a feast with my friends. Yet when this son of yours comes back after squandering your money on prostitutes, you celebrate by killing the fattened calf!"
>
> His father said to him, "Look, dear son, you have always stayed by me, and everything I have is yours. We had to celebrate this happy day. For your brother was dead and has come back to life! He was lost, but now he is found!" (Luke 15:25–32 NLT)

There are two prodigals in this parable. The younger son that had wasted all he had and now returned to reclaim his dominion. The older son had remained with his father but never realized he had such dominion. The father demonstrated this to the two sons:

- To the younger son who has returned, he said, "Welcome back to where you belong."

- To the older son who was angry at the party, he said, "All I have is yours."

In this way, the father revealed his sons to the world, and the party began. The world is waiting for the unveiling and revealing of you as the sons and daughters of the Lord. The world is waiting to celebrate you at your party. The responsibility is yours to either return and reclaim your lost dominion or come in and join in the party in the place of your dominion.

> For the earnest expectation of the creature waiteth for the manifestation of the sons of God. (Romans 8:19)

> For (even the whole) creation (all nature) waits expectantly and longs earnestly for God's sons to be made known (waits for the revealing, the disclosing of their sonship). (AMPC)

> Everything God made (the creation) is waiting with excitement (eager expectation) for God to show his children's glory completely (the revelation of the children/sons of God). (EXB)

> For the eagerly awaiting creation waits for the revealing of the sons and daughters of God. (NASB)

> For the creation waits in eager expectation for the children of God to be revealed. (NIV)

> For the creation waits with eager longing for the revealing of the sons of God. (RSV)

The entire universe is standing on tiptoe, yearning to see the unveiling of God's glorious sons and daughters! (TPT)

For all creation is waiting eagerly for that future day when God will reveal who his children really are. (NLT)

The party was not only for the lost son but also for the one that has been with the father. The father called him in to join in the party. This is the party of resurrection for the younger son and revival for the older son. Everyone celebrated.

I say to you that likewise there will be more joy in heaven over one sinner who repents than over ninety-nine just persons who need no repentance. (Luke 15:7 NKJV)

Jesus continued, "In the same way, there will be a glorious celebration in heaven over the rescue of one lost sinner who repents, comes back home, and returns to the fold—more so than for all the righteous people who never strayed away." (TPT)

There is a party waiting for you. Heaven is waiting to celebrate your return to reclaim your dominion on earth. Heaven is waiting to celebrate your discovery of dominion though you have been with the Father all your life.

And the Gentiles shall come to thy light, and kings to the brightness of thy rising. (Isaiah 60:3)

The Lord says, "Some people are waiting to come to your light." They are surrounded by darkness and living in darkness. However, when you rise, you shine." The Lord also says, "There is a brightness that your rising will radiate to the world, and it will attract even kings. The world needs revival. The world is waiting for your revival. The revival on earth is a party in heaven."

There is a party for your revival. The revival is about what you do with the dominion God has created you for. The world is yearning for change agents who will make an impact in the world for Christ, change agents who will reclaim their lost dominion, change agents who will realize and discover their dominion.

The world is waiting. Heaven is waiting. Do not keep us waiting any longer. Rise. Return. Reclaim. Come in. Join in the party. The party is for you. The party is about you. Let the party begin!

Send a revival, O Christ, my Lord,
Let it go over the land and sea.
Send it according to Thy dear Word,
And let it begin in me.

Lord, send a revival,
Lord, send a revival,
Lord, send a revival,
And let it begin in me.

Send a revival among Thine own,
Help us to turn from our sins away.
Let us draw near to the Father's throne,
Revive us again, we pray.

Send a revival to those in sin,
Help them, O Jesus, to turn to Thee.
Let them the new life in Thee begin,
Oh, give them the victory.

Send a revival in ev'ry heart,
Draw the world nearer. O Lord to Thee.
Let Thy salvation true joy impart,
And let it begin in me.

—James M. Gray

Pray along with Me

As you have read this book, I have no doubt in my mind that God has richly and truly blessed you. However, it is only when you have a personal and intimate relationship with the Lord Jesus Christ that you will get to learn more of him and from him.

It may be that you'll need to rededicate your life to Christ.

I would want you to pray now:

> Lord Jesus Christ, I thank you for your love for me. Thank you for revealing myself to me and speaking to me through this book. Thank you for making me realize your love and plan for me. I confess my sins before you. Forgive me for being selfish with all you have blessed me with. Forgive me for neglecting your word, your will, and your way. Forgive me for leaving my place of dominion and going for a wild party when you have a party waiting for me. Forgive me for being careless about my life and not realizing that I have a dominion to make and a purpose to fulfill in life. Forgive me for taking your grace for granted and not allowing myself to see me the way you are seeing me. I have returned to you, God. Please take me as I am—lonely, wounded, hurt, lost, and dead. Come now, O Lord, and take your place again in my life. I rededicate my life and surrender wholly onto you. I will never go back nor back off from you again. Thank you, Jesus. In Jesus's name, I pray. Amen.

You can now pray more unto him. Then get up, and share your joy with others. I would also urge you to read this book again and the other volumes in this series as you would get a new insight from God. You can as well obtain some copies for those you think would need this kind of revelation and encounter but either could not afford to get one or have heard not about this book. *As you do this, God bless you real good. The heaven is celebrating you now.*

However, if you have never made Jesus your Savior and Lord, I pray you will take this opportunity right now to establish the most important relationship in your life. God loves you so much that he sent his Jesus to pay the penalty for your sins with his blood and his life. And he has risen from the dead to set you free from whatever bondage. And he wants to give you a new beginning in life.

Only through him can you have a right relationship with God. Only him can reveal to you your true self. Only he can reveal to you your place and take you there. Only he can give you glory and grace. Only he can make you be what he wants to be. Only he can make you fit into his plan for your life.

God has made a provision for your salvation and healing through the death and resurrection of Jesus. Salvation is free but with a price—your willingness to accept him into your life as your Lord and Savior. Won't you receive this gift?

Please pray along with me:

> O Lord God, my father, I thank you for this that you have done on my behalf, for me and to me. As you have said in your Word that if I confess with my mouth Jesus as Lord and believe in my heart that you have raised him from death, I shall be saved. I take this opportunity to confess Jesus as my Lord and Savior. I believe in my heart that Jesus died and shed his blood for my sins, and he is risen to set me free. I ask you to forgive all my sins and iniquity and to cleanse my body, soul, and spirit from all unrighteousness. I renounce every selfish and bad past, ungodly act,

wild party, and attitude that I have lived before. And I promise, by your grace, I will never want to go back to them again. I accept your gift today. I want you to be my God, my Lord, my Savior, my Father, my King, my Friend, and my All in All.

Take my life, and make it your own, your home, and your throne. Come into my life, Lord Jesus. Come in today, come in to stay, and make my life become a home for you. Make me a new creation this day. Thank you for giving me new life. Thank you, Jesus. In Jesus's name, I pray. Amen.

I will say, "Congratulations to you, and welcome to the family of Christ." The party has begun for you. There is joy in heaven because of you today. And the joy never ends.

However, confession is an issue; you professing it is yet another vital issue. You must be a living testimony of Jesus as you also confess him.

I pray that God will fill you with his Holy Spirit as you ask him. It is the Holy Spirit that will guide you and teach you the ways of God as you submit to him.

Ask him to show you the right way to go and also to show you any wrong relationships, gathering, and wrong associations that would want to lead you into bondage and take you far from them. Also, ask him to reveal to you any wrong attitude or things in your life that may allow Satan to oppress and afflict you.

Whatsoever may be your question, Jesus is the answer.

It is vital you become a functioning part of a Bible-believing church where the Word of God is preached without dilution and compromise. Only as you are joined to other Christians can you grow and become established in your place in the Body of Christ and learn to serve others.

Ask God to show you which is which. Spend time reading and studying your Bible and other Christian literature that exposes you to the truth and not to the personality of the writers. As you do, the Holy Spirit will open your understanding and make it alive and meaningful to you. As you pray and listen to the Father, you will begin to know, and he will become your intimate friend.

Also, abstain from things that could stand as stains to your testimony—music, movies, books, friends, etc. Always bear in mind that Christianity is not a religion but living the life of *Jesus Christ* and longing to be like him. It is neither a ritual nor a routine; it is an attitude of life and the attributes of God's children. Do not struggle for position or battle for titles. Let God train, trim, teach, and place you.

Finally, share your faith with others, even with your old friends; simply tell them what God has done for you and through you. There is no greater gift that you can give your family and loved ones than *Jesus*. Let your Savoir be their Savior too.

Till we meet in my next book, remain blessed and faithful in *Christ*.

Once again, I say, "Welcome to the family of Christ." Let the party begin.

God bless you real good!

Your brother and friend,
Dr. Emmanuel Oluwafemi Olorunnisola

You can reach me by writing:
Dr. Femi Olorunnisola
P. O. Box 15065
Chesapeake, VA 23328
Email: insightreflects@gmail.com

About the Author

 When God calls out a man, he gives him a specific mission. All the man needs to do is to catch the vision for his mission and develop his passion for the vision and the mission he has been commissioned for. And God is always there to make the connections and give the provisions.

Dr. Emmanuel Oluwafemi Olorunnisola is a young, dynamic, diversified, and versatile man of God. He is a man with many unique gifts and talents, and he's using them all to glorify God and edify the Body of Christ. As a writer, publisher, poet, playwright, songwriter, singer, and novelist, he uses his creativity to make an impact in life all to the glory of God.

Dr. Femi is also commissioned with the dominion mandate to "awaken this generation to the reality of God's Word and to use all that God has deposited in them for God's purpose."

He is the cofounder and president of *Brighten Your Corner*, an organization and ministry that "Champions the charge and the channel for the young Christian leaders to let the world see the Christ in them."

He is also the founder and president of *The Leadership Fellowship*, a leadership organization that serves as a network for Christian leaders in any profession to connect, fellowship, and make an impact in the world.

Dr. Femi's writing and teaching ministry is called *Insight for Reflections*, which was established to rouse your potential and spread the revival fire. It was established "on purpose that you can discover yours."

He holds a bachelor's degree in architecture from the Ladoke Akintola University of Technology (LAUTECH), Ogbomoso, Oyo State, Nigeria. He also holds a master's degree in Christian leadership from the prestigious and highly reputable Dallas Theological Seminary, Dallas, Texas. He obtained his doctor of ministry degree in pastoral leadership from the highly reputable Liberty University.

Dr. Femi is an ordained pastor in Christ Apostolic Church and is pastor in charge of an assembly of the church—*Christ Apostolic Church, City on a Hill*, Chesapeake, Virginia.

Emmanuel is married to his lovely and beautiful wife Olasunbo, and they are blessed with lovely children. They all live in Virginia, USA.